LET THE STORM BURST

Copyright © 2020 Barry Cohen

The right of Barry Cohen to be identified as the Author of the Work has been asserted in accordance with the Copyright Act 98 of 1978.

All rights reserved, whether the whole or part of the material is concerned, specifically the rights of translation, recitation, broadcasting, reproduction in other ways and storage in data banks. No part of this publication may be reproduced or transmitted without permission given by the Author.

First Edition April 2020 in paperback

Project by New Voices Publishing Services
guiding authors to self-publish
www.newvoices.co.za

Printed by Print On Demand, Cape Town

ISBN: 978-0-620-85831-1

Let the Storm Burst

※

Barry Cohen

BY THE SAME AUTHOR

Blazing the Trail: This sport collector's volume chronicles the major impact black of golf on overcoming discrimination in South Africa and breaking down the apartheid barrier. It is a rare glimpse into the extraordinary lives of Southern Africa's top golfers (*including those who beat Gary Player and Tiger Woods*), bannings, protests, and their determination and desire to win against all odds, and ultimately, their induction into the Southern Africa Golf Hall of Fame, as well as local and international tournament statistics.

CONTENTS

BY THE SAME AUTHOR	4
INTRODUCTION	7
CHAPTER 1	9
CHAPTER 2	17
CHAPTER 3	28
CHAPTER 4	38
CHAPTER 5	46
CHAPTER 6	59
CHAPTER 7	68
CHAPTER 8	83
CHAPTER 9	96
CHAPTER 10	112
CHAPTER 11	126
CHAPTER 12	137
CHAPTER 13	145
CHAPTER 14	156
CHAPTER 15	166
CHAPTER 16	176
CHAPTER 17	185
CHAPTER 18	196
CHAPTER 19	211
AUTHOR'S NOTES	222

INTRODUCTION

Following the route of the Great Trek into the interior away from the British Cape Colony and their imperial rule, the Dutch and French descendants settled on farms in the area known as the Transvaal. Their peaceful existence was shattered in July 1886 when an Australian prospector, George Harrison, discovered a gold reef between Pretoria and Heidelberg on the farm Langlaagte. The South African Republic's formal proclamation of this discovery prompted the Witwatersrand Gold Rush and the founding of Johannesburg, which within a few years was the largest city in Southern Africa, populated almost entirely by *Uitlanders*. The economic landscape of the region was transformed overnight—the South African Republic went from the verge of bankruptcy in 1886 to having a fiscal output equal to that of the Cape Colony's in the following year.

The fledgling town of Johannesburg was laid out on a triangular wedge of *uitvalgrond* named Randjeslaagte, consisting of 600 stands measuring fifty by fifty feet. The settlement was named after two officials of the *Zuid-Afrikaansche Republiek*, Christiaan Joubert and Johannes Rissik, combining the name they shared and adding "burg", the original Afrikaans word for "fortified city".

These Uitlanders included colonials escaping the boredom of small-town life, Indians trekking from the sugar fields of Natal, the Cape Coloureds and Chinese shopkeepers mixed with Africans, eager to experience the faster pace of urban life. Artisans and miners from the gold and silver fields of the Americas and Australia, and from the coal and tin mines of Europe, joined the wagon loads of men who had learned their craft in the pits of Kimberley, while Jews in search of freedom and employment, headed south to Africa from Eastern Europe and Russia.

In 1886, Johannesburg had 26,303 inhabitants. Ten years later it was recorded that there were 102,078 inhabitants, and by 1898, the Zuid-Afrikaansche Republiek became the single biggest gold producer in the world, with a contribution of 27,5 per cent, and where the men lived rough in all manner of tents. The saloons, brothels and supply stores were made from wood, canvas and corrugated iron. It was lawless and a dangerous place to live.

But equally, it was now mainly an English community in the midst of a rural Boer society. President Paul Kruger saw this as a threat to the separate national identity of his people, "God's people," as he called them.

The law of the land provided that every white male who had resided in the Transvaal for five years could be naturalised and entitled to vote for a representative in the Volksraad.

As more and more foreigners arrived in the country to dig for gold, the government realised as early as 1890 that these Uitlanders could easily gain control of the country. The solution was to create a Second Volksraad. Uitlanders who had been naturalised for two years were granted the right to vote for candidates for the Second Volksraad. The Second Volksraad only had jurisdiction over specific matters relating to Johannesburg and the mines. Meanwhile, the residential qualification enabling Uitlanders to vote for the First Volksraad was extended from five to fourteen years, and the voting age increased to forty years.

CHAPTER 1

Africa
To the Goldfields flocked the harpies
Sordid souls from every clime
Cheating, lying, grasping, struggling
Sinking, dying in the slime
Anonymous

The sound of horses' hooves snapping dry twigs broke the eerie silence. The golden sunset caressed and painted the rider, highlighting the orange tint of his horse, while the dust shimmered in the air. The rider sighed with weariness closing his eyes, giving full rein to his horse as he swayed rhythmically in the saddle. The ground passed like grains of wood, a mixture of dark and light hues.

Everything about him seemed stationary apart from a troop of wildebeest shaded by the cool baobab, watching him, their tails swishing at the continuous hum of insects. At the same moment, the shadow of a hawk passed swiftly across the veld.

A satisfied smile mapped his creased face as he reflected upon the last few days. Hunting game had been a relaxing break from the back-breaking grind of gold-digging. He rocked drowsily in the creaking saddle, then grunted, as he gave an earthy chuckle of laughter.

As he twisted around to see if the mountain-hack carrying his skins still followed, he was hit by the whiplash-like motion of the branch which threw him out of his stirrups. His friends would have laughed had they seen him sliding groundward, clutching desperately to the horse's rump. Francois closed his eyes again and let his shoulders rock with the motion of his mount.

Dwarfed eucalyptus trees rose from the sand in clumps gathering a mound of sand and leaves about their roots as if guarding food against the wind. Those that had died still lifted their stricken limbs above the crowding suckers pushing up from below. Bare tracks in the reddish sand wound in and out of porcupine grass and turpentine scrub. Trails made by the wind twisted through the gaps in the sheltering trees. Rotting limbs and dead leaves covered the ground in the more densely timbered places.

Francois blinked, puzzled as he opened his sleepy eyes and gazed about. He frowned; the lines etched deeper into his weather-beaten face. Maybe he was imagining it, but he could have sworn he heard a girl singing. Strange, the sound was unusual in the bush.

There was a splash of water. Francois reined in quickly. Cautiously, he urged his horse forward, his gaze sweeping the bush as the rays of the sun penetrated the canopy of branches, casting leafy patterns on his shoulders.

The stream eddied lazily, lapping its banks, gurgling and rippling over pebble-strewn reaches. Shading his eyes from the last shafts of sunlight overhead, he peered through the heavy undergrowth.

A pile of staghorn moss carpeted the ground, and the maidenhair fern grew on all sides, overflowing the banks and drooping into the water all along the stream's course. Tree ferns dropped forward as though they were drinking, their wide-reaching delicate forms like giant ostrich feathers waving gently on each breath of warm air. They quivered as the ripple of the water shook their trunks.

A movement on a higher plane caught his eye. It was just the flip of a fly-tickled ear, where all else was still. The form of a kudu appeared before him as a picture thrown on a screen by a magic lantern. It stood about 50 yards from him, the soft grey and white hide looking even silkier in the shadow of the thorns. As if carved in stone, it stood still and watched, its ears catching the melodious tones that hung in the air.

Francois peered past it. A girl bathed in the river oblivious to any form of life around her. Transfixed, Francois leaned forward in the saddle, marvelling at her smooth, dusky, olive skin and her small but firm breasts. Trembling slightly, he caught his breath as he felt a rush of desire to reach out and stroke her body.

Still, he stared as her flowing long dark hair fanned the water. He closed his eyes, wondering if when he opened them again, she would be gone, like a mirage. But she didn't disappear, and he continued to stare, mesmerised.

A pebble splashed into the water, disturbing his trance. Alert, he glanced at the bushes around him, then back at the willow trees overhanging the water, his eyes narrowing. The sunlight caught the sudden movement disturbing the tranquillity of the moment. Francois froze as he saw two men edging forward.

He watched and waited as, in turn, the men each took another swig from a hip flask while eyeing the girl. With a smile to his companion, the overweight, short and unshaven man watched her, his pulse pounding in expectation at her unclothed body as the liquid dribbled across his stubble. Leering, he stared at her beautiful figure.

Francois's eyes never left the two men. He had seen their kind before. There was no doubt as to their intent.

Suddenly, in a frenzy of desire, the man charged through the water. Ripples formed a wash in his wake. The second taller ginger-haired man stayed behind, with a smile on his face, on guard, rifle in hand.

The girl, her back to him, alarmed, turned at the sound of the noise, and screamed as she tried to evade his grasp. Undeterred, her attacker's podgy hands groped at her bare breasts as he flung his arms around her. She twisted in his grip, frantic to escape as she felt his bulge harden against her.

He gripped her harder. Her strength was unequal to his as she writhed in desperation. The nail of his forefinger scratched at her silky dark triangle searching for her slit. She lashed out, yelling like a wildcat, but his vice-like grip tightened around her.

Frantically trying to ward off her attacker, she lost her balance, falling as her feet slid over the slippery, submerged pebbles. She fell back into the water with a splash, her hands thrashing, looking for a grip as she sank, helpless.

Her attacker dragged her soaked body back towards the bank. With one hand holding her down by the throat, he urgently released his belt and started to pull down his pants while pinning down her legs with his own.

A roar of anger bellowed forth from Francois. He spurred his horse through the bush. Diving out of the saddle, he hit the water, splashing waves as he dragged the attacker off his victim. He smashed the assailant to the muddy ground.

Rising shakily, pulling up his pants, the man smirked as steel flashed in front of Francois's face. Dripping water, they circled, their eyes taking in every movement. Then he lunged. Deflecting the blow, Francois was surprised by his own clarity of thought. Everything seemed as if it was in slow motion.

He ducked a second swing, but the blade tip nicked his wrist. A thin red rivulet of blood appeared. Trying to ignore the pain, Francois sank down and grabbed the man's foot, causing him to lose his balance. The knife spun from his grasp as he fell with his arms outstretched back into the river.

Francois pent-up anger surfaced as he grabbed the smaller man by his belt and jerked him upward, then forcefully shoved him forward. Off balance, the man screamed in terror, as he focused on the jagged rock as it crashed into his face. He lay motionless. Then his body slowly slid back towards the eddying stream.

Gasping, Francois gazed at the body without emotion.

The frozen picture was interrupted by the sound of snapping twigs caused by running feet. He spun around. The other man left behind on guard had disappeared as three men scurried towards him with clouds of dust in their wake.

Francois braced himself for the onslaught. He couldn't back off now. He tensed, shifting his weight in the mud as the first ran past him, halting in front of the motionless overweight man in the river. Breathless, Hammond stared, then knelt down to feel the man's pulse. A shocked expression creased his forehead.

"He's dead," he blurted out in astonishment, brandishing his firearm.

Out of breath, the others halted and gazed bewildered at the corpse.

"Put your gun down, Hammond," the eldest of the group, Phillips, commanded, his greying hair ruffled by the exertion. Hammond's grip slackened on the butt, but his eyes never left Francois.

"This woman," Phillips pointed to the trembling girl, her hair hanging in tendrils, her wet clothes clinging to her body, "has been assaulted." Now he looked at the dripping wet Francois standing on the bank. "And this man saved her."

His gaze moved over the other people who had formed a half-circle around the scene. "I propose we hold a court of enquiry."

"He's guilty as charged," Francois spat out. "He got what he asked for."

The bedraggled girl, still in shock, sobbed as she sat on the bank, her gown tightly drawn around her waist. The others gazed down at the dead man.

"He must have been drunk," Pisani muttered. "He wouldn't have tried anything like that if he was sober."

"In any case," Phillips added, taking control as he glanced from one to the other, "We must have some answers for Renzi's family."

Pisani nodded his agreement. "All right then; let's ask some questions." The tribunal faced Francois. "Did you mean to kill him?"

Francois gazed at each one carefully, while he assessed their possible strengths. He wondered whether he should implicate the tall ginger-haired man because of his involvement, then thought better of it. This was bush country. He wasn't their friend. Anything could happen here, and no one would be any the wiser.

"I didn't care if he died," he replied guardedly. "I wanted to teach him a lesson, not kill him."

"What about you, Kate?" Phillips enquired as the distressed and quivering young woman rushed into his protective embrace.

She shook as she gulped for breath. "I was bathing when I felt his arms pin me down. I didn't even hear him coming. I struggled, but," she fought to hold back her tears, "he was far too strong."

"The bastard's lost all his strength now," Francois snorted.

Phillips turned his attention back to Kate's saviour. He extended his hand. "We would like to thank you for what you did. I take it you are after a wagon. We're going to Johannesburg. Lionel Phillips is the name. That's Pisani and John Hays Hammond"

They clasped hands firmly.

"Francois du Plessis. How much do you want me to pay?"

Phillips glanced at the others, then back at du Plessis. "We won't ask for anything, just your company." A note of warning crept into his voice.

"But we don't want any nonsense with this woman." He pulled Kate closer to him. "The next man who interferes with her in any way will stop a bullet. Is that clear?"

Time seemed to stand still as Francois looked at each face. These people seemed genuine enough. Trekkers ... The interior was full of such folk with a head full of dreams of gold.

Francois grinned warmly and extended his hand. The tension eased, as everyone relaxed and smiled along with him.

"I'm glad to have the chance to come with you and transport my skins. As for interfering with this woman, I'm a member of the *Volksraad*, an honourable man. You'll have no trouble there." He hesitated, before adding as an afterthought, "I suppose you know that this trip is no picture. It's a hell of a country, with wild animals and many swollen rivers to forge."

Lionel Phillips nodded. "We know all about the conditions. I've been working as a diamond sorter for J.B. Robinson at Kimberley; Kate's a crack shot, well able to look after herself. We are equipped with mosquito nets and medicine. There's safety in numbers; the bigger the party, the less the risk."

They set off for their camp. A roaring fire crackled, throwing orange sparks into the fading sunlight as Francois and the others approached the boma. Just then the outspanned oxen moved slightly, revealing the outline of the tall, unshaven, ginger-haired man drinking from a bottle of brandy, highlighted by the fire. Francois froze. Clearly, he was the only one who recognised that this was the same man who stood guard while Renzi attacked the girl.

Phillips called out angrily as he strode towards him. "Savage! I told you no liquor was allowed when you joined the rig!"

Savage glowered back, then hissed menacingly, "Get out of my way."

He bumped his shoulder deliberately into the older, shorter man, throwing Phillips off balance. He sprawled to the raw earth.

"Why you bastard!" Phillips growled, scrambling to his knees. As if in slow motion, Savage turned and moved forward, sneering as he brandished the bottle overhead. Outweighed and outsized, Phillips backed off, the firelight glistening through his greying beard as the others gazed on.

"First, at the river and now here!" Francois shouted. "Why don't you pick on someone your own size?" His intrusion caused Savage to freeze as Francois stepped out of the shadows and confronted him.

Savage spun around; a look of angry surprise on his face as he caught sight of Francois. He slammed the bottle against the nearest rock, brandishing the jagged edges in front of him as he edged forward.

"I'll show you what happens to interfering bastards!"

He lunged forward and struck out. The jagged glass glinted in the firelight as it skimmed past Francois. The others watched, transfixed, as Francois backed off, avoiding the first few wild drunken lunges. Then, deflecting a blow, he darted forward, landing a right uppercut on Savage's jaw, causing Savage to lose his balance and his legs crumpled under him. He landed headfirst in the dust.

"Now!" Phillips commanded, "Get on your horse and move!"

Savage shook his dazed head. Slowly, he picked himself up and spat out, "I'll get you, all of you!" His red eyes darted around viciously, finally falling on Francois.

"Next time, you'll be answerable to me," Francois retorted.

Baited, Savage made a move towards Francois but thought better of it. Our paths will cross again," he cursed. "When you least expect it, mate. So, beware." Picking up his rifle, he mounted his horse and galloped off into the darkness.

CHAPTER 2

Francois stirred as the first pink flush of daylight touched the sky and felt the bite of the dew on his cheeks. He watched as the sky turned crimson with the promise of sunrise. Taking his old Martini rifle, he walked to the top of the nearest *koppie*, the crunching sound of his boots reverberating in the silence. Standing there silhouetted in the light, he saw the sun's rays fill the shadows in the hills.

A faint breeze stirred, coming from the north. This was an almost certain sign that the wind would grow stronger through the day. At one with nature, he breathed in deeply, catching the sweet smell of the African bushveld.

The orange-tinted grassland was bathed in watery sunlight as Kate emerged, still half asleep. Drawing back the canvas folds of the covered wagon, she yawned, inhaling the sweet morning air. "Morning boys," she greeted them cheerfully, passing her hand through her ruffled hair.

"Did you sleep well, miss?" Pisani looked up from his sleeping roll.

Stretching her arms sideways, Kate screwed up her face and gave a big yawn, then rubbed her sleepy eyes. "Soundly, thank you, although there was some noise in the night. I thought a wild beast was after the oxen, but perhaps it was just my imagination."

She didn't want to admit to having awakened, screaming, with the memory of the previous day's attack. But now it was daylight, and her attacker was dead. She threw her mosquito netting down, then dropped to the ground and began rolling it up.

Pisani watched her climb down. Her beauty was as young and fresh as the new day. "Wish I'd thought of bringing a mosquito net like yours," he commented, for want of something to say.

"Well, if there was more room in mine, I might have invited you all to share it," Kate giggled. Then, she blushed, realising the suggestive implications of her statement.

Lionel Phillips strolled over, carrying steaming mugs of coffee for both of them. Hammond scratched his bristly face.

"They bite like hell, they do! You people without mosquito nets should cover your heads," he advised. "I've heard that it's the little suckers that cause the fever."

"It's hard to imagine such small creatures causing a terrible illness," Kate shook her head.

"Well, it's time to get going, so let's cut the chatter," Phillips urged.

The heat rose as they trekked over the bushy veld. The wagons etched tracks into the dry earth as they rumbled eastwards to the gold mines of the Witwatersrand. The mountain slopes and gullies were adorned with trees and an array of shrubs. Drifting, Kate wondered why the sweet-tasting water of the Orange River which they crossed, was such a dark colour.

About them, the land hummed with miggies, occasionally punctuated by snorts from warthogs as interrupted, they dashed for cover. Above, cries of wheeling, twittering ploughman plovers echoed as the oxen swished their tails warding off the constant buzzing of flies. The adventurers were forced to shout "Trek!" as they flicked their sjamboks at the ambling oxen's hides.

Nearby a herd of about twenty skittish springbok stood at the side of the track, which petered out in the sand, before leaping out of sight. Among the trees, it was still and hot as they continued along the now non-existent trail. The wind had blown away most of the topsoil, leaving the area dotted with small fertile green islands in a sea of bare earth. Each oasis provided a raised platform to the wildflowers, grass and saltbush. Where the prickly pear bush had withered, sand accumulated among the dead spine. A healthy growth of barbed grass poked its head through these skeletons. Nearby a solitary shag popped up from a dive, giving them a startled glance before winging its way into the air.

Only once, as they came across two rhinos blocking their way, did Kate have to draw on the reins. The beasts snorted becoming alert, their massive grey bodies ready to charge, as they faced each other. Swiftly Francois threw some rocks over their heads, confusing their limited vision, causing them to turn and charge the clattering stones, while the trekkers pushed on unhindered.

"Well done, Francois!" Kate called, eyeing the handsome Afrikaner. As she looked at him, she felt warmth in the pit of her stomach, *did he feel the same way?* He nodded his head to her in acknowledgement. Her breasts tingled as she smiled back.

Kate felt as if the countryside belonged to her. She smiled at the flowing, floating motion of a frightened giraffe, his legs sashaying in front of him and his neck swaying from side to side as he disappeared into the bush.

This kind of land, tough, rugged and free, made one feel alive. The real Africa thought Francois. This is where families are a unit protected by the male, and their offspring guided by the females, like elephants drinking at the waterhole, with the old bull standing guard as first the females, and then their brood slurped up the coolness.

It was after breakfast a few days later that Pisani suddenly felt weak. Sweat glistened on his forehead, and his breathing was laboured. Sensing rather than feeling the approaching fever, he mentioned his fear to the others and without much persuasion from Kate climbed back into his sleeping roll and lay down in the shade of the wagon.

Some two hours later, he awoke, sweaty, and listless, with a dull ache all over his body. Kate mopped his forehead. "It seems to be the fever. I'll give him some hot bush tea to make him sweat it out."

Hammond was irritated by the delay. A revolution was coming, a new order. He had to get to the seat of government if he wanted to be part of the takeover.

"Put him in the wagon and let's push on," he ordered.

Ignoring him, Kate knelt down to check on him. Worried, she whispered across to Phillips, "He may die by the morning! His skin is getting hotter; this fever kills quickly."

Perturbed, Francois looked down at Pisani, then rapidly scooped out a trench with his bare hands. He rolled several glowing coals using a stick from the fire into the ditch and replaced the sand over the hole. "Help me roll him on to it," he asked the other men. As Pisani's shivering, sweaty body absorbed the heat, Francois spread a blanket over him.

Kate returned with a mug of fresh bush tea. She knelt down beside the sick man. "Are you feeling any better, Pisani?"

He tried to sit up to drink, but his eyes clouded, and his head throbbed. "Just let me close my eyes," he whispered. "My ears are singing with fever, my eyes ache, and my body doesn't seem to belong to me. Keep an eye on Josh." He slept.

Phillips walked slowly round the wagon, examining the condition of the wheels. His sensitive skin was already burnt by the mild early spring sunshine. Noticing a splinter, he stopped, inspected it, and reluctantly set off to fetch his tools, exclaiming with a mock tragic air. "The timing is out of joint! Oh, cursed spite that ever I was born to set it right."

Hammond laughed as he put down his steaming coffee. "Silly ass!

I reckon the fellow that said that was a waster, he chucked it."

Offended, Phillips halted in his tracks. "A gentleman by the name of Hamlet mouthed those words."

"Well," drawled Hammond with a faint smile, "I can bet he was no good anyhow." His American accent contrasted with the clipped English of Phillips.

Francois watched them both – the older, Lionel Phillips and the younger, more pragmatic John Hays Hammond. There was something commanding in his mannerism as he put his argument across.

"Just my luck is the waster's motto," Francois piped up, looking up from his coffee.

Phillips seemed unsure of his ground. "They do say he was mad, but he certainly said some wise words."

"I dare say," retorted Francois noncommittally, "a man who blames his luck is no good anyway. He's got no balls. It's not the time that's wrong, it's the man. It's not the job that's too big, it's the man who's too small." The fire sizzled as he threw his remaining coffee into it.

Considering what he'd said, Kate frowned as she poured black tea into two pannikins for the others. "You don't believe in luck at all du Plessis?"

Francois sat down again and gazed into her hazel green eyes. They had a strange effect on him. "I didn't say that." He shook his head. "But it isn't the explanation of success or failure, not by a long chalk. No, sirree, luck's just the thing a man would like to believe is the reason for his failure and another fellow's success, but it isn't so."

Kate smiled demurely and found herself examining Francois thoughtfully as he poured himself some more coffee. His hair was untidy and lank, yet it suited his rugged features with that scar over the bridge of his nose. His soiled pants complemented his well-worn shirt.

But it's those detached, knowing eyes that make you want him, my girl, thought Kate. *But I'll be damned if I agree with him.*

"Du Plessis," She tried to remain nonchalant. "Explanations aren't always excuses, and sometimes you really have to give them."

Francois stirred the glowing embers, raising a small flame that highlighted her face. He glanced down at her as she sat with her hands were clasped around her drawn-up knees. He certainly found her appealing.

"Well, you can reckon it quite sure there's something wrong with a thing that doesn't explain itself. One explanation is as bad as two mistakes. It doesn't fool anybody worth speaking of, except yourself. You find the remedy; you can leave the other folks to put up the excuses."

Taking a final sip of coffee, he tipped the remains over onto the parched earth, watching as the liquid sank into the ground. He'd made his point. Setting his mug down, he stood dusting the sand from his trousers, wincing against the encroaching stiffness in his legs and made his way to where he'd left his rifle. Then stopping, he turned and gazed back at Kate. "I reckon if that chap of yours had to keep the camp in meat, we'd all go pretty hungry."

Picking up his rifle, Francois found Josh watching him in awe. He was suddenly reminded of his friend, General Piet Otto's words: *Boys are like dogs, they've got to be taught.* "Coming along sonny?"

The picture on Josh's face was sufficient as he raced over to the fevered Pisani. "Is it okay if I go, Pa?"

Seeing the excitement in his son's flushed face, Pisani smiled. "Sure thing, boy," he whispered.

They moved off, Josh following closely in Francois's footsteps.

Nearby, Mel Savage watched and waited. He's said he would get even. Not only had du Plessis humiliated him, but he'd killed his friend,

Renzi. Savage took another swig and wiped his mouth with the back of his hand.

"What do you think we'll get?" Josh enquired, cheerfully panting as he came alongside him.

Halting, Francois looked gravely down at him. "See, sonny! If you've been used to going around like a dog with a tin, it's no wonder you've seen nothing. You've got to tread softly and keep your mouth shut."

"I'm sorry," Josh murmured in apology.

Francois studied him in silence before placing his hand gently on the boy's shoulder. "There's no bell and candle in this here play, you've got to be awake."

They continued walking, silently treading dust. Occasionally, Francois bent down and picked up pieces of earth, throwing them into the air. Wetting his index finger, he held it up to feel which side cooled, studying the breeze. Changing direction for no apparent reason, he glanced down at the ground, and slackened his pace, suddenly losing interest. "Rietbok! Heard us, I reckon."

Changing direction again, he turned at right angles and pointed to the spoor and some droppings. He gave an excited whisper. "These are signs of kudu nearby. Great for biltong." He continued straight on.

Josh glanced down at the small grouping of little dark round pellets; then alarmed, he realised that Francois had disappeared. A slight sound of crunching twigs drew his attention and he caught a glimpse of Francois moving swiftly forward undercover, stooping low, signalling with one hand behind his back.

As Josh hurried after him, there was a loud crackle underfoot as he stepped carelessly on some dry twigs. Sighing, Francois straightened, waiting for him to catch up, then looking over with a faint but ominous shake of his head. "You should have brought some firecrackers." He turned abruptly and continued through the bush.

It was a beautiful warm morning. The dew still clung to the lush, tall green grass. A gentle, cooling breeze rustled the vegetation slightly as they came out on to the veld. Turning to the boy, Francois guided him. "What would you put up for that stump?" He pointed towards a tree stump, at the same time adjusting the sights of his rifle.

"Two hundred," exclaimed Josh eagerly.

Smiling, Francois sat down. "Pace it out."

Obediently, Josh bounded off, counting out the paces aloud, but faltering as he neared the stump. "Eighty-two," he shouted, running back.

"Bush telescope, sonny," grinned Francois.

"You mean it magnifies them?" Josh panted.

"Yes, magnifies the distance like looking down an avenue! Gun barrel looks a mile long when you put your eye to it. Open flats bring them closer, and across water or a ravine, it seems you can put your hand on them."

Suddenly rigid, Francois gestured to Josh to remain silent.

Squinting, Josh peered into the bush as Francois tried to guide him. His eyes were strained and burnt from the intensity of the effort of trying to see. Still, he could not make out a living thing; the glare of the yellow grass in which they stood and the sun-splotched darkness beyond it defeated his visual acuity.

The suspense was unrelenting as he stood his ground, scarcely breathing, knowing that something was there – and that as soon as he moved, it would be gone. Then, close to the ground, there was a movement; something stirred, and the full picture flashed upon him. Through the corner of his eye, he saw Francois' rifle rise slowly. There was a long pause, then came the crack and a wild screech of alarm as the duiker toppled over.

Excited, Josh raced forward. "You got it! You got it!" Glancing back, he stopped, realising that Francois had not moved; then he grew silent as he watched him calmly reload.

Dragging the duiker along, Francois broke the silence as he looked at Josh. "It's not easy in this bush to pick up what doesn't move, and it's hardly possible to find what you don't know."

"Game, you mean?" interrupted Josh, gazing respectfully up at him.

Francois nodded and continued. "This one was feeding. I saw his head go up to listen, but when they don't move, and you don't know what they look like, you can almost walk on top of them." He smiled down at the youth, all bones and legs, remembering when he was about the same age. "Just like dogs – both got to be taught," he muttered to himself. Sitting down, he beckoned Josh to do likewise, pointing his rifle in the direction of the target standing motionless under a leafy tree.

Screwing up his eyes, it took a while before Josh saw the movement of the head of a steenbok as it cropped the grass. Raising his rifle excitedly, Josh pulled the trigger. Instantly, there was a deafening roar that made his head reel and buzz. The kick of the gun on his shoulder and cheek bruised him. When his eyes cleared, he saw the startled steenbok bound away.

Now there was more activity. There was no mistaking the kudu bull's horns once they moved. Placing his arm gently on Josh's shoulder, Francois gazed after the disappearing animal. "Next time, take a moment, aim low; don't pull, just squeeze."

Savage smiled to himself. Following du Plessis had been easy; probably concentrating on the boy had caused him to become careless, or maybe he wasn't as good as he made out. It didn't matter now; Savage was going to get even with him. He gazed down from his position, perched high up on the koppie. The frightened steenbok bounded off as the boy fired. Savage watched, then slowly reached for his rifle.

Francois halted and inspected the disturbed ground. "Pigs," he muttered and walked on. He stopped in his stride to point out where a dassie was sitting cleaning itself not ten yards off and suddenly, hearing the sounds of a clear metallic click of the lead guinea fowl he pointed to a sandy gully in front of them. Ten to fifteen guinea fowl scurried along in single file. There was silence except for the click.

A thickly overgrown swamp with tall bulrushes in the distance now became visible. Approaching slowly, Francois stopped and beckoned to Josh. Raising a warning hand, he pointed towards the gently swaying, silky reeds.

The undergrowth rustled with an odd, subdued grunt. Josh tried intently to make out the animals. Suddenly the reeds grew silent, nothing stirred. Puzzled, Josh turned questioningly towards Francois.

"They must be here; they can't have got away?"

"Try," Francois egged him on. He watched, amused as Josh rushed forward, jumped into the reeds and scrambled about.

"Pigs are like that," Francois grinned as a confused Josh returned. "Same as elephants, they just disappear, unless ..."

Savage raised his rifle as du Plessis came between his sights; a smile creased his lips.

"Unless what?" Josh questioned.

Puzzled, Francois gazed about. "Unless someone or something is disturbing them. It couldn't be us because we are downwind." The rising sun momentarily reflected a glint of metal high up on the koppie. Instantly Francois threw himself at the boy.

Savage tightened his grip on the trigger as Francois remained in his sights. He squeezed. The click of the firing pin echoed as it hit the chamber. The rifle roared, simultaneously the cartridge expelled from the breech spun to the ground.

Just as Francois bundled the boy over, the bullet whined ominously past. "Stay down!" Francois shouted.

Josh remained frozen, too shocked to dare move as Francois looked up with caution. Rising slowly, he helped Josh to his feet. "Come, son."

They made their way up to the koppie where Savage had lain in wait. Francois examined the ground. Picking up an empty whisky bottle, he sniffed it then gazed off over the veld following Savage's tracks in the distance. They caught sight of a rider galloping briskly out into the *bundu*.

Who had tried to kill them? And why hadn't he shot a second time? Francois suspected it might have been Savage, but where was the proof?

CHAPTER 3

The fire roared into the open sky, throwing sparks into the air as it crackled and hissed. The party sat near its warmth and protection, enjoying their coffee. High above, billions of stars in the Milky Way across the southern sky glittered and twinkled, watching protectively over the adventurers as Kate coaxed on by the others began singing.

If all young men were hares on the mountain
How many girls would take guns and go huntin'?
If all young men were rushes a-growin'
how many girls would take scythes and go mowin?
If all the young men were ducks on the water
how many young girls would undress and dive after them?
But the young men are given to friskin' and foolin'
So, I'll leave them alone and attend to my schoolin'

Laughing, they whistled their approval, adding snide comments which Kate returned with interest, sending them into fits of laughter. Phillips handed around more coffee as they continued to sit and stare into the roaring fire, relaxed and at one with their surroundings.

As more wood was added, the fire gained life, lighting up the veld for a few more yards. A hyena howled at the added glow and withdrew a few paces so that its eyes shone in the darkness.

"You may all be a bit late in finding workable claims, but the population of the valley is continually changing as unsuccessful miners leave. Still, the whole area is a potential gold mine," commented Francois as he oiled his rifle.

Hammond fiddled with a twig, drawing pictures in the sand. "I expect they work night and day at it?"

Francois stared fixedly into the dipping, swirling flames darting upward and outward in the breeze. "No, not at night, and never on Sundays, though many foreign agitators would like to, contrary to the President's decree. It's a funny life," he continued, glancing at their attentive faces. "When a miner decides that his claim is finished, and no more gold can be found on it, he may sell or just move away and forget it. Then a new arrival takes his place and suddenly strikes gold."

He saw their dreamy eyes imaging what it would be like when they discovered shiny nuggets hidden in the dust and dry dirt. What an exciting and elating feeling!

Kate leaned towards the warmth as the twigs she had thrown into the fire smouldered. They grew silent, lulled by a feeling of comradeship.

Intrigued, Josh watch Francois meticulously oil the rifle barrel. "Did you ever shoot a man, *Oom*?" he asked at last.

No sonny, never had to use it yet," Francois replied without looking up. He could feel the boy's eyes watching him. *The admiration feels kind of good*, he thought to himself, as he smiled.

"It looks very old." Josh still curious, commented, "Have you had it long?"

"Just about fifteen years, I reckon," replied Francois, now opening the barrel as he pushed a piece of cloth through it with an iron rod.

"Seems like a long time to carry something without using it," Hammond interrupted after overhearing the boy's question, taking on a challenging attitude as he stared across at Francois.

"Well, that's so." Francois bit his lip. "It's a thing you don't want often, but when you do, you want it damn bad."

Kate studied Francois closely. His curious indifference towards her was a bother. She wondered whether under that sprouting beard and lank hair he really was as cool and unflappable as he appeared. Still, she pondered, there was a certain warmth in his clear blue, now reddish eyes, reflecting the glowing fire.

How long had he been watching me bathe before stopping Renzi? He must've seen me naked, but then maybe he hadn't. Still, she felt a tingle run through her body at the thought of Francois relishing her nudity. "What's the best thing to do when following a wounded buffalo?" she chipped in, trying to gain his attention.

"Get out!" replied Francois bluntly.

"Yes, but what if there isn't time?" Kate persisted.

"Say your prayers," muttered Francois, still not bothering to give her his attention.

"No, seriously – what is the best way of tackling one?"

His smile took some time to develop. It moved over his face slowly, reminding Kate of an egret in flight, as if the wings had come and gone. "If you want to know," Francois replied, now looking directly into her eyes, "there's only one way; keep cool and shoot straight."

"Oh, of course," Kate replied flippantly, "If you can."

"And if you can't, best stay right at home," he answered.

The night closed in, and there was quiet once more. The flames of the campfires died down; the big thorn logs burnt into glowing coals like the crisp pink hearts of giant watermelons.

Morning came. The sun beat mercilessly upon the adventurers, sapping their energy as they kept well in the shade. All except Kate, who was too preoccupied with a romantic novel for the heat to bother her. It riled her that Francois had put her in her place. He had got the better of her, for now, but she was as good as him in every way.

And, dammit, she was going to prove it!

Lionel Phillips glanced up as she made her way purposefully over to him. "Mr Phillips, before going to daddy's farm in Lydenburg, can't I go with the diggers to Johannesburg and try my luck digging for gold?"

Phillips examined this slip of a girl. "Those men are rough diggers." He smiled in a fatherly manner, glancing at the soiled, bearded men around them. "They wouldn't relish having to look after a woman while they are panning for gold." He shook his head. "Hell, I doubt whether there'll be another respectable woman in the camp!"

Kate had already thought the argument through and was ready with her answer. "I won't remain at the digging indefinitely. I only want to see the place. As far as I know, there isn't too much hard work involved. And I'm strong, as fit as some of these men." She glanced at the overweight Pisani. "Even if I stay there only a week," she pleaded, earnestly peering into his eyes. "It's a gamble without having to risk anything."

Phillips pondered the idea, his fingers slipped idly through his greying hair. Loose women were the only ones he had known at the diggings, and although she had her father's fiery spirit, she certainly wasn't one of those. Still, it wouldn't do any harm if she was there for a short while.

"Well, I'll see," he replied as he looked thoughtfully across at du Plessis sipping his coffee. He rubbed his hand over his stubble chin. "Let's ask du Plessis his opinion. He knows what the conditions are like, as he lives at the diggings."

Du Plessis glanced up startled lost in thought as Phillips called him by name. For a moment, his eyes locked with Kate's.

"Du Plessis," Phillips asked, "How do women fit in with the diggers at Johannesburg?"

Francois became aware of Kate hovering. Her slim, neatly trousered figure complimented her fresh, honey-tanned face. He wondered what her motive was.

"Well, one or two of the miners have built shacks in the village overlooking the river and have their wives with them." Francois paused as he reflected. "Up to now, it's been a pretty rough life for women, but those already there are of farming stock and used to hardship."

Now he searched both Phillips' and Kate's faces, frowning slightly. "Those diggers are not as wild as you might imagine. There's justice for all, and public opinion is the most effective force everywhere. There are, of course, many idlers but they are kept in their place, for while justice may be halting, it's apt to be short and sharp." He glanced enquiringly from Kate to Phillips. "May I ask what's on your mind?"

"Kate wants to remain at the diggings before going to Lydenburg." Phillips raised his eyebrows.

"Do you think my idea is wrong?" Kate interrupted. "Surely there's no danger in me just looking?"

Francois stared at her with amusement. How would this attractive girl be able to handle the attention of the men, let alone dig for gold?

"No, you'd be perfectly safe," he smiled, shaking his head.

"But I can't imagine you digging and picking away at rocks nor working a sluice bore. It takes strong men to keep it up for hours on end. Once you've opened up a claim, you must stick at it until you get to the granite rock bed where the gold is lodged!"

"Then I'm going to join the diggings if you don't mind," replied Kate stubbornly, her hands firmly fixed on her hips. Francois scratched his head and grinned, impressed with her determination. "Well, I really don't know. I never heard of a young lady trying her hand at that game."

Kate looked quizzically from Phillips to Francois. "If I can persuade Mr Phillips here, that's exactly what I'm going to do."

Something told Francois that Phillips had already lost the battle.

The sky and mountain parted from some remote embrace. Pale and exhausted, the dividing range detached itself from a bed of blue and stood erect upon the horizon. They watched it gain in strength, increasing in size. From pale blue, it changed to azure and then to tawny green.

The buttressing spurs, seemingly offering their strength to support the mountain, sprawled towards them, their exploring fingers lost in the scrub of the foothills. Deep watercourses like ribs grooved the sides with pools of shadow lying in the valley at their feet. The oxen strained with lowered heads as the wagon rocked, sometimes leaning alarmingly sideways when the camber of the road increased to meet the bend.

The hills they traversed were not very steep. Still, even then, the pole straps pushed the collars around the oxen's ears, and the single bar banged against their hocks as they strained back to check the gathering speed as they moved down the sloping hillside.

At the top of a rise, guarding the foothill, Kate reefed in the oxen to give them a breather. The path dropped away before them then hugged the deeply ridged side of a hill. It disappeared behind the crest of each spur, only to reappear lower down, still supported by the bank of earth cut from the side. The trekkers gazed at the hill in gloomy silence. If they got down there safely, they'd get anywhere.

Francois lifted a tent pole from the back of the wagon.

"The idea," he said, handing it back to Pisani, "is to rest it on the side of the floorboard and lever the end against the rim of the wheel. That's if she starts to bolt."

"What if the end slips into the spokes?" asked Pisani, somewhat unenthused about the idea.

"In that case, the other end breaks your jaw, or mine, or both." Francois retorted seriously.

"It'll be yours," Pisano joked as he grasped the pole, holding it in readiness.

They started off at a walk that turned into a jog. At the first bend, they were striding. The oxen began to plunge as the heavy wagon thrust them forward, skidding and spitting out rocks and dirt from the wheels as Kate reefed on the reins. She pulled the oxen back until they were hard against the single tree.

The brake handle was pulled back to the last notch as Pisani thrust the end of the pole against the rim of the front wheel where it clattered and screeched in anguish as his hands jumped and shook to the kick of the vibrating rod.

The fact that nothing could be seen through the dust before and after, further confounded them, so that only bitter oaths and cursing could be heard.

The collars of the oxen were dangerously close to being forced over the animal's heads, and Kate loosened the reins to enable them to keep their grip on the ground. They swayed into a gallop as the chatter of Pisani's stick turned into a scream.

Hammond hung onto the oxen while the unwieldy wagon rocked like a ship on a stormy sea. They tore around the last bend like a stagecoach pursued by masked bandits. The oxen raced ahead to avoid the front wheels that could sandpaper the hair from their hocks at every stride. Then, suddenly, the gradient levelled off, and they were again on the straight.

A sigh of relief rippled through the party.

"Thank heavens that's over!" Phillips seemed shaken as they slowed to a walk. *Having lived through that, surely nothing worse can happen to us?*

The dry perspiring heat became more oppressive. It was relieved by an occasional late afternoon thundershower which drenched yet cooled everything. The rest of the journey was surprisingly trouble-free except for the wheel mount breaking off as the oxen hauled the wagon through another dry riverbed.

About them the veld abounded with frolicking, leaping game as they pushed on, breaking camp at dawn, halting only at dusk and trekking through the rugged countryside. They tried to keep as close to the recognised trail as they could, travelling half the time by instinct and the sight of previous trekkers' discarded possessions.

The party was in high spirits as they halted at yet another Sotho village. Dark brown children rushed out to meet them. Their brown eyes bulged in excitement as they clung to whatever scant clothing hung loosely about their bodies, beads jangling and flying in the air. They stopped a few paces from the wagon staring at Kate in amazement and then clustered excitedly around her.

Now the women followed, stroking Kate's long flowing hair in awe, clicking their tongues in their own language, while others fingered her loosely cuffed trousers and smooth white skin. Backing off, the bare-breasted women giggled shyly as their men emerged from among the grass thatched huts.

Pisani, perched on the wagon with his chin pushed out in a superior manner, surveyed the prevailing scene. Seeing this, Francois smiled deviously to himself and decided to have some fun. Rummaging first through his saddlebag, he made his way over to the wagon, clambering alongside Pisani, filling his pockets with sweets. He whispered, pointing towards a group of nubile bare-breasted girls gathered a short distance away, giggling among themselves.

"Now, you go and give them a few sweets," Francois innocently smiled. "And if they don't astonish you with their delight and gratitude, I'll really be mistaken."

Pisani scrambled off the wagon and ducked under the spindle bar. He sauntered over to the girls with an air of innocence, putting his hand into his jacket pocket and withdrawing a sweet. He gave it to the first girl, who grabbed it eagerly, clicking her tongue furiously as she called to the others.

There was no hesitation on the part of the other girls as they made a quick dash for Pisani and grabbed at his jacket pockets. Shocked, Pisani managed to draw out a handful of sweets despite their clawing hands. Desperately he emptied his pockets and threw the sweeties beyond the girls' reach. They rushed like mad in a flurry of bare brown legs as they scrambled to fetch the delicacies.

"The last time I was here," chuckled Francois, "that big girl over there picked up my friend Jimmy and cleared off with him right into the village with all the others in hot pursuit."

"So, you expected to see the same again, you bastard," panted Pisani angrily as he reached the safety of the wagon.

"Sure did," laughed Francois. "I made certain of it as soon as I saw her come straight for you ... And by God, here she comes again."

Pisani shrank back from the sight of this Amazon who was intent on carrying him away to give him her own brand of appreciation. "Do something, Francois, for heaven's sake!"

"Hand me your mirror, Kate," Francois called, then spoke to the Sotho woman in her own language. She smiled and held out her hand. Absorbed with the shiny circle of glass in which she could see her own reflection, she lost interest in Pisani. Seeing her own face was far more exciting.

"All it takes is a little bartering" Francois still chuckling.

"For sure I'll get you for that." Pisani still panting mopped his brow.

The others howled with amusement.

CHAPTER 4

Johannesburg

Excited, they rose before dawn and were greeted by a mildly warm morning. They were now near the goldfields. With each passing minute, the sky seemed to brighten as if someone was turning up the oil lamp. The dew still weighed down the heavy-topped grass with clusters of crystal drops that glittered like diamond sprays. Eagerly they packed their gear, removing the stored billy cans, spades, picks and other mining equipment from the wagons.

Nearby, a little red rietbok got up and shook the dew from his coat, stretched himself, then picked his way daintily through the wet grass, nibbling here and there as he went.

Beaming, Kate made her way over towards Francois, who was tightening the strap of his saddlebag. "Behold, a gold miner!" she exclaimed excitedly, holding her spade aloft. "At least I'm going to the village to see if I can be given a claim. If so, I shall try my luck for a short while." An impish smile of delight and expectation spread across her face.

Francois couldn't help but grin in return. Her enthusiasm was infectious. "Who knows, maybe fortune will smile on you, and you'll strike it rich?"

Blackbirds carolled, merging their melody with the voice of the bush. Nearby, the soil was pitted with the diggers' holes alongside mounds of gravelly clay discarded by gold-besotted miners. The loveliness of the morning crept through them like a drug as they set off down the koppie. The tinkering sound of men picking at the earth punctuated by the occasional laugh or greeting echoed through the air as the town rose and once again began the endless search for gold.

Living conditions were harsh and alienating. Canvas shelters appeared before them, sprouting like toadstools after the rain, fossickers' holes and clay heaps, some protected by awnings. The only wooden buildings were made of packing cases. Dismal-looking iron shanties intermingled with mud-heaps. Wells and washing apparatus by the scores were everywhere on view. As they progressed, the tents became more numerous, and unwashed diggers popped their heads out to see them pass.

They occasionally stopped to watch the bearded, grimy men burrowing feverishly like moles into the earth, scarring the face of nature. The air was filled with discordant shouts of men and the noise of the cradle as they rocked it, shovelling in mud and gravel, and then washing it down.

The trekkers made their way down the solitary gravel road past three or four iron gold-buying shanties, past Height's Hotel, the wooden double-storey saloon and the corrugated iron bank. Before them, rows of tin and wooden makeshift shacks appeared.

Francois responded with a broad smile or wave in response to greetings of almost everyone they passed as comments relating to Kate were bandied about. She savoured the men's approval and responded warmly to their whistles by nodding and grinning.

After reigning in outside the Gold Commissioner's shack, Francois dismounted and entered followed by the others. Making straight for the map fixed onto the wall, he thumbed it purposefully.

"You see, you must first register your stake." He gestured at the map. "There are a few that have been abandoned. You could claim on them after we've checked here." He watched the expressions of eager anticipation spread across their faces as they savoured the prospect of finding gold. "Five shillings for each licence and it just might make you a millionaire."

Adjacent to Francois' claim, the Pisanis ardently set about learning the mechanics involved in digging for gold. The process required that the dirt be sifted continually, twisted and turned in whorls until that faint speck of gold appeared gleaming in sharp contrast with the ochre earth. Initially, the diggers could perform the work themselves, using relatively little equipment.

Meanwhile, Hammond continued with his journey, examining the diggings alongside the main reef, the soil and clay, and contours of the land. All the while, he took copious notes as he surveyed.

Nearby, Lionel Phillips roamed, searching for a suitable claim. Kate, having been left in the care of Pisani, watched for a while, then got restless. Spurred on by the prospect of finding gold, she grabbed a pick and hacked at the granite rock bed alongside Francois and his dark aged friend Joseph. Many of the diggers paused in their back-breaking task to watch this lady at work.

After a while, Francois wiped the sweat from his brow with his palm. Leaning on his pick, he grinned at her growing embarrassment, chuckling as more and more diggers arrived to stare at her. "They'll soon get used to you."

It was a while before they had collected a pile of loose gravel and stones. Kate sifted the earth. An expression of disappointment showed on her face as she saw that no traces of gold were visible.

Suddenly, a delighted shout indicated this was not the case with Pisani, as he peered at the specks of gold in his sieve. Holding the fragments up to the sun, "Isn't that a glorious colour!" he whooped.

It was a chaotic time in Johannesburg with its share market in turmoil after a potential disaster was discovered in the mines. Nevertheless, days progressed into weeks, and still, Lionel Phillips hunted for a decent claim. Diggers seemed to flood every inch of that barren stretch of earth. He passed by gentlemen directly out of Eaton, Oxford, and Cambridge, decked out in Bushman khaki, with the indispensable stock whip in their hand and short, black clay pipes in their mouths. They spoke with a variety of accents, and there was a universal language, that of greed.

Other, more experienced "old hands" wore corduroys or buckskin trousers stuffed into durable boots or bound by leggings and a red or brown jumper. Their bundles of blankets or skin rugs were rolled around a few items of clothing, from their belts dangled sjamboks and knives, and in their hands swung blackened quart pots or billies. Tarpaulin tents slung over sapling frames formed an adequate camp, and leaves or rushes served as makeshift beds. Most contented themselves with fire-blackened porridge, and cold mutton washed down with black tea.

Eventually the number of diggers dwindled to an occasional tent and Phillips reached the outskirts of the town. He turned to retrace his steps. *There certainly is no gold here in this barren scrubland*, he mused, as he gazed over the savannah. In the distance, a figure of a man became visible. *Odd,* Phillips thought, *he looks familiar.*

"Well, I'll be damned!" he exclaimed with a grin. "It's George Farrar! What brings you here?" he shouted as Farrar approached.

Farrar's leather boots were cracked and broken, and dust clung to his once white, now grimy shirt. His eyes twinkled as he jested. "Cor blimey, where've you been mate?" he asked jokingly, his Cockney accent heavy and grating. "Last I heard of you, you were half dead of the Lowveld fever! How are you now?" Phillips asked, then grasped Farrar's outstretched hand.

"I survived," Farrar grinned.

Phillips moved back a pace from the odour and Farrar's dusty, ragged appearance. "You've walked a bloody long way, all right."

"And what do I do when I get here?" Farrar winced, "Work twelve hours a day for someone likely as not will not be able to pay me at the end of the month!"

Phillips smiled, marvelling at the fact that here in the middle of, well, almost nowhere, he should bump into an old friend. He shook his head in amazement.

"You found anything yet?" Farrar asked.

"Still looking for a workable claim," Phillips explained with a shake of his head. "Still there is some luck around here. A bloke told me a couple of days ago about finding nuggets. Thousands of quid in one hour off one claim!"

"I should be so damned lucky," Farrar started walking.

"It has to happen to some of us," Phillips smiled.

Together they gazed at the distant hive of activity.

Placing his arm on Phillips' shoulder, Farrar jerked him, puzzled, as he pointed towards a strange, shimmering contraption in the distance. "Lionel, what's over there?"

Phillips stared in that direction. "That's Welgespruit, Fred Struben's place. What you see there must be the new five-stamp battery that arrived for him a day or two ago. I hear he's got a heap of reef there waiting to be crushed. Reckons he'll make a fortune out of it. They tell me he's having a devil of a time getting the battery erected. Nobody except Fred himself knows how to put it together."

"A five-stamp battery," Farrar whistled. He put his hand to his forehead and shielded his eyes from the sun's glare as he gazed at the metal rafters and huge linked chain. "That's one hell of a big mill for a place where there isn't supposed to be much gold."

They both looked at the silent mill. Around them, the ground hummed with life as the sounds of the diggers' grunts of exertion reverberated through the veld.

"George," Phillips turned to Farrar, "We can put a battery together. How about it? Should we give it a go?"

"Not me, mate," Farrar replied with a shake of his head. "That sort of stuff's not my line. Digging, sure, bricks and mortar, yes; but clambering up and down those girders? No, thank you."

Phillips grimaced, shrugged his shoulders and slowly retraced his steps towards the diggings. "Actually," he commented, halting in mid-stride, "I know somebody who's looking for a mason. If you go to Langlaagte, the widow Oosthuizen wants to put up a house for her son. His name is Hendrik. She is Petronella, I think. But she's the one with the money. So, go and see her."

"Sounds like a good proposition to me. Tell you what, Lionel; you go over to Struben's place and I'll go and see the widow. Then if you don't get fixed up, come to Langlaagte. If there's nothing doing with the woman, I'll join you at Struben's."

"And if we don't see each other for a bit, we know we're both at work."

"That's it," Farrar acknowledged, then took his leave. "No use mucking about here. I'll be getting along. You know where to find me, so stop by for a drop of whisky."

It was some days before Phillips ventured out to Langlaagte. The veld was still fresh and damp from the afternoon shower. Butterflies in soft yellow, white and green circled around him as he made his way to where Farrar was baking bricks, the partly built house taking shape behind him.

He fell, but not into the stride he had intended, but over a boulder concealed beneath the lush grass. Cursing as he sprawled, the dust powdering his cheek, angrily he gripped the dislodged piece of rock, dashing it down against another stone, then made as if to kick it. He hesitated as a yellow glow blinked back at him. Curious, he gazed down, then snorted. "Iron pyrites, that's fool's gold. Can't fool a digger anymore," he muttered.

Puzzled, he bent down and picked up a chipped piece, scrutinising it. Suddenly it flashed in the sunlight. Scrambling around furiously for further segments, he studied each piece with mounting excitement. Then holding a lump in each hand, he ran towards the house where Farrar, a trifle perplexed, had been watching his antics.

Examining the piece of rock critically from every angle, Farrar gave a low whistle.

"Have you ever seen anything like it?" Phillips blurted out.

"Can't be gold! Must be pyrites!" muttered Farrar, shaking his head in disbelief.

"I tell you, it's gold!" Phillips shouted. "You think I can't tell the difference by now?"

"Well," Farrar commented, "I've never seen this amount in a reef before. But we can soon find out. Show me the exact spot."

Phillips pointed to the rocky outcrop. "Let's take some more samples, then crush and pan them. Get your hammer and any other tools."

"We'll find something," Farrar glanced around. "There's always plenty of junk lying around."

They took turns at chipping away, reducing the heavy mass to a mixture of gravel and powder. Breathing heavily, Phillips looked up. "Now what, how do we pan it?"

Farrar grabbed his frying pan. "We can make a few kinks on the side. That'll do the trick." He hammered away, then tipped the crushed rock into the pan while Phillips tipped his water bottle over the pan. He straightened up as Farrar, bending over the pan, began to wash the dirt, swirling it in a circular motion.

They both held their breath as Farrar tipped out the last cup of mud-saturated water. Their heads nearly collided as they peered intently into the pan.

"God Almighty!" Phillips whispered hoarsely, puncturing the silence.

"I've never seen anything like it. Not here, or Australia or California!" Farrar muttered as Phillips tilted the pan from side to side. A thin trail of shining specks of gold glistened against the mesh.

CHAPTER 5

Francois' eyes adjusted to the dull interior as he entered the Gold Commissioner's shack. Grinning, he stared down at his friend. Pisani lay arms outstretched, chained to the floor, his clothes torn and tarred. The blood stained his newly grown moustache as he tried to smile through swollen lips.

"I hear they've locked you up for assaulting a policeman," Francois chuckled. "How did you get into such a state?"

Pisani shrugged his shoulders. "Had a bit too much to drink, hammered him, and he clubbed me back."

Francois hovered over Pisani still grinning, amused at his discomfort. "Okay, I'll go and see the Commissioner."

"Thanks," replied Pisani, relieved. "Incidentally, Kate said to tell you she's leaving for her father's farm. I heard your friend Savage is going along for the ride. She doesn't suspect."

Francois paled. It wasn't just Kate's departure, but the fact that she was to be accompanied by Savage which made him scowl. Turning, he stormed out, Pisani's shouts echoing after him. He strode down the muddy road, his six-foot-two frame taking on the appearance of a charging bull as he headed for the hotel.

Kate replaced her teacup as she watched his approach from the veranda. Savage smiled to himself as he relaxed in the canvas deckchair, savouring the moment.

Beaming radiantly, Kate rose to greet Francois, her eagerness causing him a certain amount of confusion. They stared at each other for a long moment, the silence unbroken. Then Kate gestured at her companion. "You remember Mel Savage. Well, he's been kind enough to volunteer to ride all the way to Lydenburg as my escort," she smiled. "I had hoped I could get you to join us."

Her persuasive tone disarmed Francois for a moment. Then he pulled up a chair.

Savage stared scornfully at du Plessis. An impudent, challenging grin played around the corners of his mouth, as he purposefully let his eyes wander lustfully towards Kate. A static silence crackled as Kate sensed the animosity between the two men. She well remembered their fight around the campfire. She tried to break the tension. "So, what do you say, Francois?"

"I'd like to go with you," he replied. "But if I leave my claim for any length of time, someone's bound to jump it. And as it's still very much a paying proposition," he paused as he added, his tone softening, "I hope you'll come back and stay for a while."

He glanced down the road. "There are several women living in the village now, and the place is growing all the time." He stopped, then asked abruptly, "When do you leave?"

Kate was troubled by his rebuff. "Depends on when I can get a seat on the mail-coach. The hotel manager is going to make arrangements for me. I should know today or tomorrow."

"I'm quite willing to ride with you, miss," Savaged butted in. His smile disarmed her as he slipped his arm about Kate's waist.

Francois glared coldly at him. "I'm not sure Kate is all that keen on your company Savage." His fists clenched.

Kate removed Savage's arm, trying to defuse the strain between the two men. "Mel's been digging near Pilgrim's Rest with his brother. They've been reopening some old mines there," she quickly changed the topic to more neutral ground.

Savage took the rebuff lightly. He smirked as he lounged back on the sofa. "How are you doing on your claim here?"

"Showing a small profit." Francois reply was curt.

"Maybe I'll come here and try my luck." Savaged bantered. "That is after I get back from Lydenburg."

"No more room here now," Francois retorted, clearly annoyed. "More diggers than claims."

"Oh, I expect I'll get by, mate." Savage laughed. "Anything for a change of scenery." An awkward threatening silence enveloped them as the two men faced each other.

Francois was the first to turn away. He had more than a bellyful of Savage. Now he faced Kate. "I'll come tomorrow around noon, maybe we can have a meal together?"

Savaged wasn't going to be denied the last word and rose, inserting himself between Francois and Kate. "Say, do you mind if I come along and see your claim?"

"No one but me sees it." The reply was offhand.

"Ah, I won't pinch any of your bloody gold, mate!" Savage needled him.

"No!" Francois looked fit to explode. "All claims look alike. Just go to the nearest one, if they'll let you!" Francois stomped off.

Smiling triumphantly, Savage shook his head as he faced Kate. "Bad-tempered one, isn't he?"

"Surely you know that diggers never tell you whether they're doing well or not?" Kate defended Francois, annoyed at Savage's provocative manner. "They don't talk about what they find. The surest way to annoy him is to ask questions about his claim."

"Maybe that's why I did it." Savage got up and ambled away.

The following day the hot African sun blazed down, burning the digger's already bronzed flesh. The heat added to Francois' ill humour as he made his way towards the hotel. His mood heightened as he spied Savage sprawled in a chair on the veranda, a half-empty whisky bottle on the table nearby.

Spying du Plessis, Savage grinned, flashing his tobacco-stained teeth as Francois came abreast of him. "Roses are red, violets are blue, pickles are sour, and so are you," Savage chortled as he baited his man. "Say, what are you doing here, you bad-tempered old man? You going to call on the little lady?" He wagged his finger. "Better not, 'cause I've included her in my plans, and nobody interferes with those, mate!"

Ignoring the contempt, he felt for Savage, Francois did not reply as he continued towards the stairs. He merely walked around Savage, giving him no more than a casual glance.

Savage waited until the last moment before thrusting his leg outward. He caught Francois' left heel, sending him sprawling headlong. Heaving his bulk off the ground, Francois did not hesitate as he threw himself at Savage, kicking and punching. The chair where Savage sat toppled over. Dazed, Savage tumbled off the veranda into the road. Furious, Francois leapt after him, as the two men scuffled in the dust.

Diggers spilt out of the doorways and rushed up the street crowding around them, shouting advice as they watched the spectacle.

Francois gritted his teeth as he aimed for the bastard's jaw. Savage ducked, and then swung a powerful right into Francois' gut, causing him to sink breathless to his knees. Again, he aimed his boot into Francois' back.

"Fight with your fists, man!" Pisani shouted from among the assembled, ragged crowd.

"My fists will more than do the job," Savage gloated at Francois' discomfort as he waited for him to rise. Francois got to his feet, sucked in his breath and launched his attack. But Savage struck him first, drawing blood from Francois' mouth. Again, he hit him, opening a cut across Francois' nose. Confident that his opponent was dazed and beaten, he turned towards the crowd, right fist aloft, leaving his left side unguarded for a few seconds. This was enough time for Francois to step forward. He snapped Savage's head back with two left hooks and a powerful straight right into his left eye.

Savage counterpunched, swinging wildly, his vision now blurred as he missed with a right. Again, Francois caught him, causing blood to stream from his nose and mouth. It dribbled off his chin.

Kate, attracted by the cheering, emerged onto the veranda. Angrily, she ordered them to stop. Ignoring her, Francois connected with a wild flurry as Savage wrestled him to the ground. Francois rose and tore into him, his fist connecting with Savage's good eye.

Hardly able to see now, Savage's blows became wilder and more vicious. "Where's the whining bastard?" he bellowed, "lemme put his lights out!"

A straight left to the jaw finally silenced him as he crashed to the earth with a thud.

Bruised and bleeding Francois caught sight of Kate's horrified gaze. Without even attempting an explanation, Francois glared at her, and then walked off. A nearby digger threw a bucket of water over Savage.

Some days later, a still bruised Francois unearthed a large nugget. As he licked it, it shone brightly. He shouted out, quite excited, holding the gleaming irregular shape aloft. "Pisani, look what I've found!"

"What weight do you reckon it is?" Pisani dropped his pick and rushed over.

"Eight ounces," guessed Francois as they examined it.

"Let's have a drink." Pisani uncorked his hip flask and passed it over to Francois.

Taking a swig, he gazed down at the nugget and shook his head in disbelief. "At first, it was just a glimmer, then it shone brighter as I pulled it out."

"It's an incredible feeling."

Pisani took another swig. "Better than fooling around with girls, hey, Francois?"

Francois' gaze was troubled. "I wasn't fooling with girls, just one—and then maybe I wasn't really stringing her along."

"I don't know," Pisani grinned. "When you have enough of this stuff, you won't need to chase them because they'll come running after you. It's far easier that way!" His gaze became dreamy, "I remember once when I was in the money ..."

"The kind of girl you can buy with cash wouldn't be for me," Francois interrupted. "Although I must admit being rich opens so many doors."

"Well, most people are forced to get along without it," Pisani admitted.

"I think," Francois turning over the nugget in his hands, "I'll take it to the bank."

"Why don't you call on Kate and explain the reason for the fight?" Pisani's question was quizzical. "If she doesn't want to listen to you, then that will be the end of the business."

Francois considered the idea. "I might just do that."

Kate sitting on the veranda felt dejected. Her tea grew cold as she faced Lionel Phillips, quite troubled. The brawl had horrified her, especially since she was the reason. It didn't matter if Francois was to blame; she hadn't meant to drive him off and wondered whether he would forgive her now that Lionel had explained what Savage's real intention had been. To think that she had been ready to ride with him to Lydenburg after he had been party to her attempted rape!

"I'm only on leave from my father's farm." She looked worried. "He'll expect me back sometime soon."

"It's time you got married," replied Phillips with fatherly concern. "Let your husband look after you."

Kate blushed profusely. "I can't just take a fancy to any man and then ask him to marry me!"

Phillips spread his hands in an expansive gesture. "There are at least fifty young men in this camp who'd be happy to have you, not to mention me." His laugh was nervous. "But you keep us all at arm's length."

"I don't want all those men." Kate smiled at the thought of being so desirable.

"Now you are being facetious," Phillips ticked her off. "You know what I mean!"

"I do." The blush persisted. "But I am not in an easy position. I know that if I wanted to, I could get married soon. But, to me, marriage seems the end of freedom. Maybe I'm just not ready to be tied down."

Phillips understood her confusion. "I think you are. Just don't wait too long. Time flies and takes youth with it." Then he asked the question that had been at the back of his mind for some time. "What about du Plessis?"

Kate looked flustered. "Francois is like an old friend." Now the blush spread to the roots of her flowing hair.

"Well, he surely doesn't act like one." Phillips shook his head. "He behaves more like a suitor towards you. Once that claim of his has paid off, he'll be worth a great deal."

Kate lapsed into an embarrassed silence, trying to still her thudding heart.

"Now I'm talking like a father," Phillips spoke kindly. "Is he dragging his heels? Would you like me to prod him into action?"

A horrified expression flittered across Kate's face and her breath quickened. "Oh, goodness, no, don't do that, please! We're just good friends. If you suggested such a thing, he'd probably pack up and run for his life."

Phillips studied her beauty. "You are very modest, my girl. I cannot imagine any man in his right mind fleeing from you."

She seemed not to hear him. Her eyes were fixed on a figure coming towards the hotel.

"Well, speak of the devil!" Phillips chuckled, then rose quietly and disappeared.

"Hello, Francois," Kate called gaily as he approached.

"I thought that maybe you wouldn't want to see me again," he replied, pleasantly surprised as he drew up an empty canvas chair.

Kate responded with an air of innocence as she opened her eyes wide and pouted. "You weren't the only one to blame for that disgraceful scene." Now she leaned forward and passed her hand gently over his cheek. "I see that your face is bruised."

Francois thrilled to her touch; his heart started to hammer. "When are you going to Lydenburg?"

"I don't think I want to go back there," Kate replied, her eyes fixed on his. "The farm is so far away from anywhere. It's just a house surrounded by land. I just don't want to spend the rest of my life there."

Francois felt awkward and ill at ease as if she were the first girl he had met. His breath quickened as he reached out across the table and touched her warm hand and felt her respond as she slowly stroked his fingers. He smiled at her as their hands entwined. "You must take a walk up the valley to the claims again. Pisani and Josh will be pleased to see you." *Why did he talk about them now?*

"And what about you, aren't you glad?" She grinned as she withdrew her hand.

"You know I am," he stammered, wilting under her gaze.

"All right," She smiled. "I'll tell you what. If you like, I'll prepare a meal at your camp while you go and fetch them."

The fading sunset threw a soft pink blanket over the veld. The men had ceased their digging for the day. They were now moving back to their tents and huts where evening fires spread a smoky haze over the flat veld. Others were down among the canvas stores and flimsy structures of rickety buildings where flags flew above a wild kaleidoscope of costume and race.

Pisani, Josh and Francois, resplendent in clean white shirts, with neatly combed hair and polished boots, strolled over towards the shack. Kate embraced each of them warmly as they entered. Suddenly she stepped back, her expression one of horror. "That awful thing is coming off for sure!"

Pisani recoiled from her gaze. "What on earth are you talking about?"

"That horrible *thing* growing there," she hissed, pointing at his newly grown moustache. Her feigned horror now gave way to girlish giggles. The others, too, pealed with laughter as Pisani fingered the hairy growth and looked sheepish.

She pointed to their neat attire. "It's a compliment which I appreciate." She slipped her arms through Josh and Pisani's. "You all seem like brothers to me."

"I'd rather be a suitor," Pisani responded with the directness of a man not used to courting women.

"I can't very well marry all of you." She smiled. "It's against the law."

Pisani withdrew his arm, reached into his pocket and produced a small gold nugget. He offered it to her. "This is for you, from me."

"It's a lovely gift," Kate replied, somewhat overwhelmed. "I shall keep it always." She kissed him gently on the cheek.

"It would make a perfect wedding ring," Pisani stammered.

Her answering smile was enigmatic. She did not commit herself either way.

Neither of them saw the relief on Francois' face.

Pisani now watched as she stoked up the fire and stood the saucepan back on the coals. Her movements were competent, her arms and legs firm. "That's enough, thank you, Kate," he responded politely, as she dished up succulent venison and crisp potatoes.

Her voice rose an octave. "What's the matter with you, anyway? You really don't need to be shy. There's plenty of food. So, no nonsense from any of you, now!" She filled the plates. Each man began eating without waiting for the other to start.

"We've got a mouse in our camp," Pisani commented halfway through the meal. A twinkle lit his eyes, and a mischievous grin creased his face.

"Heavens, that's nothing," Francois retorted, winking back at him.

"Yes, but we are keeping ours. He's earned himself the right to a place in the camp." Pisani returned the wink as they both turned and faced Kate.

"How come?" she asked, puzzled as she fell for the bait.

"Well, you see," began Pisani. "This mouse was more of a pest than most mice. Every time I opened a cupboard, there he was, gnawing at something, sitting up on his hind legs, and wiping his whiskers. At night he woke us up by running through our hair." Pisani now chewed on another forkful of venison, then carried on, noting that Kate seemed entranced by his tale. "Hell, I tried every dirty trick to catch the pest, but the wily fellow avoided me every time. So, after a while, I just gave up. Until one day, I just reached out and grabbed him by the tail. Hell, it was a mean trick, but he was taking so much for granted."

"What did you do with him?" Kate, wide-eyed with astonishment, piped up.

"Well, I took him to the edge of the cliff," Pisani continued. "Then I swung my arm three times and threw him as far as I could. You won't believe this, I know, but the little bugger landed with a bump, then scuttled back to me. He came so fast; all we could see were tracks in the dust. Then he scurried back up the cliff, ducked between my legs, ran into the shack, then made a beeline for the cupboard where he began gnawing again. After that, I just had to leave him alone." Pisani concluded, barely managing to control his laughter. Francois spluttered over his beer, unable to keep a straight face.

Realising she'd been had, Kate grabbed her fork and flung it at Pisani. "Did you think I'd fall for that!"

He saw it coming and ducked. It clattered to the floor. Kate picked it up, and then she too started chuckling.

"I think I'll check on my equipment." Francois rose and indicated to Pisani to do likewise.

"Oh, well I might as well come with you," Pisani said casually, rising from the table. "Stretch the legs, you know."

Outside, stumbling in the dark, they made for the cask of wine stored behind the shack. "We have to siphon it out." Francois inserted a thin rubber hose. "I'll stick it in the bung on the topside of the barrel. You suck it to start it flowing."

"Hmm, it's good," Pisani murmured, as he drew in the sweet liquid.

When he stopped, a few droplets escaped his lips and glistened on his chin.

"Whoa!" Francois interrupted, taking his turn with a long gulp. Then he exhaled deeply and passed the tube back to Pisani. "Here, try some more."

Now reeling slightly, they staggered back inside. Kate immediately noticed their strange behaviour as they laughingly made their way back to the table.

"What's the matter with both of you?" she asked, annoyed.

Pisani wanted to reply that he was fine, but the wine now churned with his food in a sickening combination. His face turned a deathly pale. Mumbling an apology, he rushed out and vomited up the entire contents of his stomach. The sand became cloyed with half-digested bits of food and frothy, red liquid.

Kate heard the sounds of Pisani being sick, but she did not intervene. She just waited anxiously at the door. Could it be her carefully prepared food that was causing him untold misery? No, it wasn't possible! She didn't feel queasy. Both Francois and Josh seemed all right.

Pisani then returned. He saw with a wry grin that Francois had carelessly put his fist through the crust of the pie that Kate had just spent an hour baking. He grinned at the red-faced Francois, who now gesticulated behind Kate's back, indicating that Pisani should take her outside while he tried to repair the damage. Pisani took her arm.

"Are you all right now?" she asked, still somewhat worried that it might be her fault.

A choking sound erupted from behind her as Francois tried to swallow his giggle. Sensing something wrong, Kate spun round. She saw his glazed look and then smelt his breath. Now she understood where they'd disappeared to and what they'd been doing.

"Get out!" she screeched; the pleasant evening ruined. "Stay away from me, you brutes! And don't ever come back!"

CHAPTER 6

Days passed into weeks became months. With the onset of autumn, the nights cooled, and mornings became wet with dew, but the days stretched sunny and clear. Meanwhile, lean shopkeepers, doctors, lawyers, runaway sailors, deserting soldiers, even self-ordained diviners and strong-minded females in ultra-bloomer costumes gathered like flies around a treacle butt. The town expanded with these new arrivals seeking their fortune. They worked at their respective claims, rising at six, toiling until midday, and then continuing after a short break.

One hot, dusty day, Francois found himself talking to Pisani as they stood outside the bank in the middle of the main Johannesburg thoroughfare. About them, the town buzzed with the news of the arrival of Barney Barnato, the Kimberley diamond magnate and member of parliament.

While they waited, Francois regaled the story of Robinson.

"So, Hans wanted to sell his farm where gold had been found for 20,000 pounds. Hearing this, Robinson rode to the farm and offered him the 100,000. Hans accepted. So, Robinson took out two bags of coins. The first contained 100 pounds, and the second, 1,000 pounds. Then counting it out into two piles, and pointing to them, he announced, Oom Hans, here stands one hundred and there's a thousand. Together, 100,000. Believe it or not," Francois chuckled, "Hans accepted."

Pisani roared with laughter. "The silly bugger!" The noise of the crowd around them suddenly rose. Francois knew that the important visitor had arrived.

"He's finally here," Pisani commented. "Your old pal Barney, the great Barnato. Such a surprise."

"He hardly gave his agent time to organise a welcoming committee this morning." Francois remained motionless, staring at the crowd as they made their way past on the opposite side of the road. Newspapermen buzzed around Barnato, trying to extract information.

Barney Barnato, only five foot three, wearing thick-rimmed glasses, grew up in the Whitechapel slums of London, the grandson of a rabbi. A strange, yet likeable Cockney fellow. He left England for Kimberley to join his brother Harry when just a slip of a lad aged seventeen, with the object of making his fortune. When he arrived in Cape Town, he had five pounds in his pocket. He could not afford the coach to get to where the diamonds had been found and ended up walking all the way with a bullock cart that was delivering supplies to the miners. It took him three months to walk there.

Arriving penniless at the Kimberley diamond fields in 1873, he became a *kopje-walloper*, a diamond buyer. He would go from claim to claim buying a stone here and there and then sell it for a small profit to the diamond buyers in the town, using his poor eyesight and youth to entice ignorant diggers into believing they were getting the better of the deal.

Eventually, he had an opportunity to buy a claim. Initially he went into partnership with Louis Cohen, his cousin and journalist (whose very funny satirical book *Reminiscences of Kimberley* later caused an uproar when it discussed the unsavoury dealings of certain mining magnates, such that J.B. Robinson sued him for libel causing him to be declared bankrupt). Within ten years, he was a millionaire. The Barnato Diamond Mining Company that he helped establish was a competitive rival of Cecil John Rhodes' De Beers diamond company.

Consolidation of adjacent mines became Barney's goal. Cecil Rhodes, the brilliant but somewhat myopic expansionist, working the De Beers mine, had the same idea and became a major competitor in the race to merge the separate mines. Finally, Rhodes proposed that they combine to form one new monopolistic consolidated company, De Beers Consolidated Mines.

In 1888, after much hard bargaining, the Barnato brothers sold out to Rhodes. They became the largest shareholder in De Beers for the astronomical sum of £5,338,650, purported to be the largest cheque ever presented for payment at that time. Barney, just fifteen years after arriving penniless in Cape Town took home £4 million (*around £4,9 billion today). After that, he became Kimberley's member of parliament, while Rhodes was appointed the Prime Minister of the Cape Colony. Investing in the Rand now became the Barnato's highest priority.

Meanwhile, two doctors, MacArthur and Forrest, invented a new process for extracting gold from the ore using cyanide. It was possible to extract ninety-six per cent of the gold from the ore, using this process. Barney ordered the necessary equipment to be shipped from England to set up a cyanide plant for each of his mines.

Additionally, he invested in all manner of infrastructure that he knew would be needed for the future growth of Johannesburg. He purchased land in the new town, building offices, shops and market stalls, including a new stock exchange.

Making royal progress from the Heights Hotel, Barnato walked along jauntily, his immaculate frock coat swinging away from his narrow white striped trousers. He wore a white carnation. His butterfly collar was poised over a gleaming silk cravat, and the leather gloves matched his shoes while his gold-rimmed pince-nez magnified the sparkle in his eyes. His full waxed moustache contrasted against the rosiness of good health and success.

As he doffed his hat in a magnanimous response, he revealed hair parted straight down the middle, falling like eaves on each side of the dome of his forehead. A man made durable by diamonds, substantial by gold, and formidable by personality and courage.

"Well, aren't you going across the road to meet him?" Pisani asked, surprised by Francois' reticence.

Francois held up his hand. "Not me. He'll probably cut me dead anyway."

"But I thought you were old friends?" Pisani probed.

"Let's just say, I know him too well." Francois ambled away. "Like a brother, perhaps. But that's not it. He asked me to go down to Kimberley to help him in the elections. I wouldn't do it, so he won't forgive me."

As Barnato blazed along Commissioner Street towards the stock exchange, a trail of men attached themselves to his wake like asteroids to a comet. Nine out of ten of them tried to sell him something. At the corner of Simmonds Street, he was stopped by a barrier of people and a row of wooden posts set across the intersection. Above the head of the men who closed around him, he caught a quick glimpse of Francois. His bright blue eyes beamed with merriment as he pulled out a pocket-handkerchief and wiped his hands and face.

"Francois du Plessis, you old bastard! Come here!" Barnato shouted. Ignoring the crowd surrounding him, he elbowed his way through them and embraced Francois warmly.

"Get me out of here before they rob me," Barnato pleaded. "Where can we go for a drink?"

Francois grinned, and clapped his smaller, slightly eccentric Jewish friend on the back as they made down the road, leaving the crowd of well-wishers in their wake.

Barnato and Francois brushed past two well-wishers like schoolboys as they laughed, nudging each other.

"You wouldn't do nothing for me in the election," Barnato berated him. "You are bloody ungrateful! You should really have stuck with your old friend. Still," he grinned, "I beat those Kimberley bastards." The expression on his face became smug. "Nobody wanted me in. Not even Rhodes, though he was on my side. He had to be." A frown creased his brow. "I know he doesn't like me. He looks down on me 'cause I've never been to college like him, and I'm Jewish." He pounded one fist into the other. "But I sure as hell beat him in Kimberley. He had a stone in hand, but I won at a canter!"

Barnato, effervescent and full of chatter, wiped the sweat from his brow with the back of his hand as they walked. "Tell me, Francois, who are the individuals doing the most business here?" he probed. "Who are the people I'll have to deal with? Not just shares, but property, mines, everything."

Drawing out his thick, steel-rimmed glasses from his breast pocket, he clumsily fitted them, then unfolded his newspaper to search the share columns. "Ah, lemme see, FitzPatrick, Bailey... That's a new one for a start. He's got a list of about eighty mining shares. Who the hell is he, Francois?"

They passed the White House ignoring the greetings from the friendly girls who had entertained them in the past. A dog yapped, snapping at Barnato's trouser turn-ups.

"Abe Bailey came from Barberton," Francois explained. "Bright fellow. Beginning to launch out in other directions. I should think he's worth keeping an eye on."

"All right," Barnato's eyes questioned his. "So, there's Bailey. Who else?"

"Your old pals, Robinson and Beit." Francois went on.

"Oh, yeah." Barnato grinned, waving his hand like a wand. Then he rattled on. "They don't like me up here, especially that crooked bastard, Robinson. Having me around upsets their little apple cart. I know them all too well. Still, I'll leave them alone for the time being." Now he turned to Francois. "What about all those square heads? Lillienfeld, Hanau—a decent chap, that one. The Lippert brothers. I'd like to give their red beards a twist."

"They all involved in concessions," Francois put in.

"What a way to make a living." Barnato sniggered. "Bribery and corruption for a solid month, then no more work for the rest of your life. Blooming theft by false pretences, that's what it is. Wish I had a few," he added with a wry grin.

"Don't we all?" Francois agreed.

The door swung back on their hinges as they entered the pub; a few heads turned in their direction.

"There's going to be hell to pay about that dynamite monopoly," Francois commented as he drew up a stool. "Lippert got the government to grant him exclusive rights to manufacture dynamite in the republic. In fact, they say the bastard's got the government in his pocket."

"Yeah, I know them all!" Barney rambled on. "Even Kruger." Then he seemed to tire of the subject. "How are you getting along? Honest, tell me. How's your boxing?"

"Oh, I have plenty of money." Francois smiled. I'm doing quite well. As for boxing, that ended quite a while ago. I'm too old now, so I just have the occasional workout."

"That right?" Barnato exclaimed, raising his eyebrows in mock surprise. A mischievous grin now played around the corners of his mouth. "So, you've got plenty of money, eh? You owe me a tenner! Red Rum, the bloody nag lost, still running!"

Francois jabbed a questioning finger at himself in mock surprise, but before he could say anything, Barnato interrupted. "Yes, you do! Don't talk so much. You must always pay your racing debts. You mustn't put other dues against it." He punched Francois lightly on the arm. "No excuses, you lost."

"Tell you what," chuckled Francois. "Forget the bet. Come and eat with me. There's a young lady I'd like you to meet."

Sitting on the hotel veranda, Phillips gazed down the dusty road as yet another covered wagon full of excited newcomers entered the town. Turning the page of the *Daily Digger*, Farrar took another sip of his whisky, and then read on. Suddenly, he turned to Phillips and thumbed the newspaper advertisement as he read aloud. "Mel Savage, recently arrived from Australia, on hearing about the boxing ability of Francois du Plessis, champion of Johannesburg, would like to fight him in any style he likes for 1,000 to 5,000 pounds a side. Savage hopes du Plessis will rise to the challenge and defend his title." Farrar put down his newspaper.

"Lionel, this Savage is good! I knew his uncle well. One of the shrewdest men in Australia, he was. Savage is staying in that place opposite Height's Hotel. Go around and see him. Assess what shape he's in." Farrar cleared his throat. "Tell him I'll guarantee his purse. He'll need a backer or two if he's thinking in thousands. Du Plessis won't be short of backers, as Barnato's bound to have a go." He sniggered. "I'd like to take a couple of thou' off Barnato."

Phillips set his drink down slowly as he gathered his thoughts. He knew who and what Savage really was. "Look, George." He wagged his index finger. "I know of Savage's record; he was in the wagon coming here. He's fought most of the best men in England, but he's a bad one. Francois and I had a lot of trouble with him." Phillips was hesitant.

"Francois is a friend of mine, I wouldn't like to see him beaten in a boxing contest, not after what went on between them."

"Well, Lionel, let's leave that part of it to du Plessis. If he's as good as Barnato says he is, I don't see what you've got to worry about." His gaze shifted to the newspaper; he turned the page and took another sip of his drink.

The gym reverberated to the sound of blows thudding into the leather punching bag as Barnato and Francois rubbed their perspiring bodies down with crisp, clean white towels after a light sparring session.

"Do you know this fellow, Savage," Barnato enquired. " Is he good?"

Francois continued rubbing himself down with a towel, ruffling his hair. "Came across him more than once. Tried to hunt me down once, just missed. We've already had two punch-ups. As a boxer, I hear he's got a useful record. I'll find out more about him from my mates." He looked thoughtful. "Out of my weight division, as he must be a couple of stone heavier."

"About the challenge," Barnato asked, draping his towel over the ropes as a boxer in the ring pounded his opponent. "Shall we take him on?"

"We, Barney?" Francois looked at him curiously.

"Certainly." Barnato grinned as he pulled his shirt over his head. "I'll back you if you're willing to fight. I've got a pretty shrewd idea where Savage will find his stake money."

Francois shook his head uncertainly as he considered the proposition. "Well, you know that I've announced that I'm finished with prize fighting, but I know what they'll all be saying if I refuse the challenge! Never mind the score I have to settle with him. Hmmm ..." He trailed off in thought, then scratched his head. "How much are you willing to put up, Barney?"

"Good man." Barnato slapped him on the back. "I was sure you wouldn't spurn this opportunity!" He grinned. "Tell you what we'll do. I'll get a couple of pals, and they can tell Savage we're willing to put up 2,000 pounds to his 2,500. Winner takes all." The magnate's eyes gleamed with excitement. "Now let's work out a reply to this challenge."

Francois continued skipping rope as Lionel Phillips entered the gym. Phillips paused to watch two youngsters sparring, then sauntered over to Francois. He greeted the boxer with a grin and stood to one side watching a while as the arced skipping rope swung around continuously. "Look here, Francois," he interrupted. "I've decided I'm not going to have anything to do with this fight because I couldn't possibly back you. The other man is sure to win. If that's the case, I'll have no bet."

Francois continued puffing, perspiration dripping down his forehead as he stopped and stared at Phillips. "I've got a good chance. I'm still in good shape. Hell, I need backers Lionel!" Francois shook his head. "He's not fit. Neither is he built to be fast. He's got nothing below the waist. You can be sure I'll fight the bugger and beat him!"

"What about the weight difference?" Phillips asked.

The heavier he is, the slower he'll be," Francois said. "And the better I like it, but then don't tell anybody!" A momentary silence elapsed. He saw that Phillips was unconvinced and nodding, he added, "If you won't back me, why not back the other man!" He rubbed himself down. "What are the latest odds?"

"Six to four against you, and evens if you can get it."

Francois raised an eyebrow. "Then why not have a good bet on him at evens and have a saver on me? Though I'm warning you, you'll make more money the other way round."

"Well, if it's all right with you, Francois." Phillips looked determined. "I'll go around and back my fancy. But I don't like it, not at all."

CHAPTER 7

The air was full of expectation. The weather was wonderfully warm between thunderstorms. The present, fun and the future full of potential. Dogs barked a good deal more than necessary. Rare and precious donkeys brayed their self-importance, and so, perhaps, did too many humans as the town buzzed excitedly in anticipation of the late afternoon boxing clash.

Banners draped the main road as diggers milled around discussing both boxers' chances. The majority of bets favoured Savage as more and more ox wagons arrived filled with families of farmers and diggers alike. Meat sizzled on open braais as men turned the spits. Nearby, podgy women gossiped in small groups, their puffy, long dresses billowing outward like sails in the breeze. Young girls paraded in their Sunday best, trying to attract the attention of the boy of their fancy while their fathers watched them like hawks.

Hendrik Vorster reefed in his oxen as the wagon creaked to a halt. He helped his plump, tiny wife, Tienie down to the ground. She was followed by his equally fat, pimply daughter Mariana. He surveyed the scene around him, as his other daughter, Karina, a smooth-skinned and dark-haired fourteen-year-old poked her head out of the wagon. She smiled demurely at a nearby group of boys. The slim, striking girl with a developing figure and attractive smile brought an instant reaction of whistles from the boys.

Amused, Kate watched Josh's face as he stared at her, spellbound. Kate smiled and draped her arm around the lad's shoulder. "There's a load of dynamite."

Josh grinned and looked wistfully up at Kate. "She's the most beautiful girl I've ever seen."

Before Josh could move, muscular Pieter van Niekerk, one year Josh's senior, approached the wagon to assist Karina down. He firmly placed his arm around her and drew her momentarily against him. Their bodies touched, and her firm young breasts were squashed up against his chest.

Kate felt Josh tense as Karina broke free from the boy's grip. "Bide your time, my boy," she warned. "You can't fight Pieter van Niekerk yet. She's already seen through him; he's only got good looks. With her feminine guile, she'll use him to provoke all of you into declaring yourselves."

Another youngster, Le Roux, moved forward towards the wagon and approached her father. "Can I give you a hand, Oom Hendrik?" he inquired, smiling at Karina and making sure she'd heard him as her father outspanned the oxen.

"Well, that's very kind of you, my boy," Vorster replied, chuckling inwardly. "Yes, you certainly may."

Breathing heavily, van Niekerk watched le Roux angrily. Then he noticed Karina staring at him. Squaring his shoulders, he made up his mind. He walked up to le Roux and tapped him on the shoulder. "Herman le Roux let's settle this once and for all. The winner gets Karina." The menfolk nodded their approval as the rivals battled it out in the time-honoured way.

Van Niekerk had a more powerful punch. It was all over in a few minutes. After a few quick jabs with his right fist, le Roux fell back in the dust. Blood spurted from his nose. Van Niekerk stood above his rival, a gleam of victory in his eyes. Now, as he moved towards Karina, there was no disputing that he had earned his prize. A smile played over Karina's mouth as she greeted the victor. Nearby, the other young girls whispered together, flaunting themselves, jealous of the attention being paid to Karina. The elders chuckled, and some began laying bets as Oom Hendrik looked on.

The afternoon's sporting events saw Josh win the pillow fight, then end up equal top shootist. In the horse race, he derived much pleasure beating van Niekerk. He ignored Karina's admiring gaze as she now focused her attention on the winner.

As the late afternoon Boere-dancing continued, Karina constantly remained within sight. She kept glancing at Josh, but he took no notice of her. Eventually, the last dance was called, giving the boys time to choose their partners as they got ready for the final whirl. The musicians fiddled, banjos strummed, and the accordion squealed with high-pitched *boeremusiek*.

At last, Josh approached Karina with a slight smile. It was time to test her interest. Out of the corner of his eye, he noticed van Niekerk make his move. They stared at each other defiantly, before returning their attention to Karina, who flashed a furious look at Josh. She chose van Niekerk and walked off with him onto the dance floor.

Van Niekerk turned abruptly and faced Josh. 'Run along, little boy," he sneered, a grin of triumph etched into his spotted face. He then turned his attention back to Karina; she had made her choice.

The music stopped, and the men started making their way towards the fenced-off enclosure. They were in a state of excited anticipation for the big fight. All except Josh, who remained standing until he picked out van Niekerk from among the crowd. Approaching him, he called out loudly. "Van Niekerk!" He beckoned him to come closer. Then before his rival could gather his wits, Josh ran full pelt, butting his head into van Niekerk's gut. He groaned loudly and doubled over in pain. Josh then gave him three rabbit punches to the back of his bowed neck. Van

Niekerk keeled forward to the ground, groaning, his eyes unfocused.

Now Josh returned to Kate, a satisfied grin all over his face. Kate put a tentative hand on his mouth.

"You men! Really!" she scoffed. "Of course, you would have had me to deal with if you hadn't smacked that upstart. Josh, I've been talking to Oom Hendrik, and as you seem to be smitten with Karina, he's invited you to visit them." Kate put her arm around his shoulders. "Josh, the man who marries his daughter gets 1,000 acres of the best grazing land and about a hundred head of cattle. Naturally, he wants to know more about you."

"But, Kate," Josh interrupted, somewhat taken aback. "I'm not interested in getting married."

"You must, one day," she replied in a motherly fashion. "No reason not to mark out where you'll sow, then in three years you'll be ready to plant." She ignored his shocked look. "So, tomorrow, after the fight, you ride with them. Your father has arranged for Joseph to ride with you. When you think you are going to make a fool of yourself, take his advice as though it were ours. And remember, it's not for you to promise anything. That will be attended to afterwards." She hesitated, before adding. "You are not to lie with the girl, either. You understand me?"

Embarrassed, Josh smiled sheepishly.

Kate couldn't deny that he was handsome. His body was lithe and lean, he hovered on the threshold of his first sexual experience. It was hard to deny the urge she had as she pressed him closer to her.

"Karina's older than her year, and hot as pepper," she whispered.

Josh grinned back at her. "I know."

"I can tell that, for sure," she responded with mixed feelings.

A huge crowd of assorted townsfolk assembled around the boxing ring. The excitement was palpable in the clearing out at Eagle's Nest. An enclosure 100 feet square built from corrugated iron nine feet high kept out the expected crowd of spectators who wouldn't be willing to pay the entrance fee.

The shadows lengthened in the late afternoon sun. Padded canvas had been spread over the straw-covered wooden floor. Three strands of rope were bound around the four wooden corner posts, with makeshift logs and stumps for seating surrounding the ring. The excited jabbering increased as the fenced-in enclosure started to fill up.

"Farrar, your man's too late," Barnato berated him. "If he's not here soon, we'll claim the fight and the stake money."

Farrar, resplendent in green pants and a red shirt, stood his ground arrogantly, protecting his man. "Yeah, and you'll get yourself lynched if you do. Anyway, Savage turned up before four and went away again. It's du Plessis, who's late!"

A loud splintering followed a roar outside, caused them to stop their bickering. They spun round in time to see a hole appear in the fenced enclosure as diggers spilt through, elbowing and pushing other diggers aside.

Phillips and Farrar reacted immediately, running towards the hole as they tried to prevent non-paying diggers from entering.

"Don't be a fool, Farrar," bellowed Barnato. "And you too, Lionel. We can't lick that lot! They'll trample the place down and us with it. Let enough of them in to keep the rest out, and we have them on our side."

"Barnato's right!" Farrar shouted, catching hold of Phillips. "We can't fight that lot."

Entering the ring amid much cheering from the assembled diggers, Francois led the way, wearing green shorts and a white vest. He was followed by Savage cloaked in red and wearing black shorts. Their fists remained bare as Barnato rubbed his own jelly substance over Francois' knuckles. From across the ring, Savage took another swig from a whisky bottle.

Hammond flipped a coin, and Farrar called heads. The shilling spun, then headed groundward, tails up. Choosing the left corner nearest town, Francois changed position, walking over to Savage, who remained stationary and glared menacingly at him before being led off by his supporters.

Tension showed on Barnato's face as he rubbed Francois down. A flow of words poured from him as he tried to encourage and psyche him into a winning frame of mind.

"If you last ten minutes, I think we've got a good chance."

"The crowd roared 'Start the fight!'" The baiting was led by Rogaly, a young, fiery Irishman with a loose tongue and a shock of red hair. He shouted from among the diggers congregated around Francois' corner. "You look pale, Francois! Are you scared, laddie?"

Francois smiled and pointed towards Savage. "Not me, I'm afraid for that bugger after I've finished with him!" The diggers nearby roared their approval as Hammond busily drew a line across the centre of the ring. He pointed to it.

"This is the scratch. When time is called after each round, you men have to toe it." Sending the combatants back to their respective corners to disrobe, he faced the volatile audience.

Holding his arms aloft, Hammond beckoned to the festive crowd for silence, then began the introduction.

"Gentlemen, we have assembled here today to witness a contest for the championship of all the South African Republics between Mel Savage of Australia and Francois du Plessis of Johannesburg. The selection of officers and all other arrangements have been carried out to the satisfaction of the combatants. We have a strong corps of press representatives." He pointed down towards the left neutral corner where a group of men with rolled-up shirt sleeves were busily jotting down their introductory notes. "I can only hope that there won't be any necessity for these gentlemen to note any unfair action."

"There bleeding will be if you don't stop jabbering and get on with it," Rogaly retorted. This led to an immediate howl of laughter and much mirth from the congregated diggers as Hammond tried to continue.

"The stakes fought for today are the largest that have ever been contested in the world." A ripple of wonder could be heard in the crowd. "I shall now introduce Francois du Plessis of Jo'burg." He pointed towards Francois, who raised his arms aloft in response to the cheers of the assembled diggers.

"...And Mel Savage of Australia." He waved a hand at Savage, who grinned. His handlebar moustache twitched as he raised his arms, parading around the ring to a mixture of boos and cheers. He clenched his fists at the hostile diggers.

"May the best man win!" Hammond turned towards the combatants. "Gentlemen, I wish you both luck."

Kate's heart raced as Savage and Francois slowly approached each other. They refused to shake hands; coldly, they stared at one another, much to Hammond's chagrin. Savage sneered at his opponent before returning to his corner.

Barnato bathed Francois down with an oily sponge as they waited for the fight to commence. A galvanised washtub being struck emitted a loud gong as Hammond called. "Time!"

The fighters sprang out of their respective corners like coiled snakes. Francois reached the scratch first as they toed the line impatiently, fist held high. The gong struck again.

Savage moved forward quickly, unleashing a wild rush at Francois' body, who countered with a left, catching him flush in his face. The force sent Savages' head whipping back. The crowd cheered their approval. Again, Savage circled, and then rushed in, only to be countered with a solid right to the bridge of his nose. Dazed, he faltered. The sudden look of surprise on his face was heightened by his eyes blinking rapidly as his head reeled with pain.

Irritably, he rubbed his nose. "I ain't come here for this kind of thing, mate," he hissed as he glowered at Francois.

"First blood," roared the crowd, as Francois' blow connected, leaving a cut under Savage's eye. Savage stood back, hands on his hips and laughed at him. Francois picked him off again with short, stinging, jabbing lefts, to the noisy cheers of the crowd. Savage now continued with his wild rushes, trying to use his weight advantage. He drove forward with all his weight and power to bulldoze his opponent, who dodged quickly, but couldn't avoid the blows altogether.

They clinched, then Savage head-butted him. As Francois backed off, a blow caught him on the shoulder with enough force to knock him to the ground as he slipped. Kate gasped. Instantly, Savage held his hands overhead as he turned his back on Francois and approached Hammond. He acknowledged, "knock-down allowed!"

Barnato quickly entered the ring and helped Francois back to his corner. Has he stunned you?" he asked with concern.

Francois shook his head, momentarily confused. "Yes, a little, but it's passing. Fuck, he bit my ear, but don't worry, I'll float out of range like a butterfly next round."

Barney sighed, relieved. "Take it easy."

The gong sounded, and time was called for round three.

Rushing off his stool towards the middle of the ring, Savage beckoned to Francois as Barney held him back, giving him more time for his head to clear.

"Hi! Send your man up here!" Savage gestured from the centre of the ring as Hammond again shouted, "Time!"

Francois moved to the centre as Savage struck out again, causing him to continue to dance away and avoid all his attempts without retaliating. Infuriated, Savage crossed to the centre of the ring and folded his arms angrily. "I say, mate, guess it looks like we're here for sprint racing; what say now if we do a little fighting for a change?"

The crowd chuckled. They were hungry for some real action. The fight continued. Low blows rained on Francois, causing him to go down in the fifth round.

Suddenly, an exhausted Francois dropped to the ground.

"Down without a blow," Savage protested.

"Quite fair," Hammond retorted, ignoring his objection.

Savage pushed Hammond angrily aside, and then bent menacingly over Francois. "Oi, du Plessis, stand up and fight like a man."

Then abruptly, he turned and made for his corner while Barnato helped Francois up. Francois sat in his corner trying to catch his breath, while Barnato worked feverishly on his bleeding knuckles.

Continuing amid the rising excitement of the spectators, rabbit and kidney punches were landed in the infighting by both men. Savage began to take the upper hand, his extra weight an advantage. An excited Farrar shouted to Barnato, "Didn't I tell you!"

Savage kneed Francois viciously in the groin, causing him to drop his guard as he staggered. Angry chants of "shame, shame", swelled forth from among the spectators.

"Shut up!" Savage held up his hand in an obscene gesture.

"Go in and smash him!" Farrar screamed.

Savage did what he was egged on to do. He punched Francois like a man possessed, trying to floor him. Blood seemed to stream across the ring in slow motion landing on the patrons.

Barnato hauled him once more to his corner and ended the round. Working frantically, Barnato waved the now blood-red towel in front of his man cooling him, at the same time encouraging him. "Man, you're doing fine. Another smack like that and the fight is over. I'm telling you; don't you understand?"

In his corner, Savage took another gulp of whisky while Farrar rubbed down his perspiring body.

The gong sounded. Exhaustion now was evident on Francois' face. He remained on the stool, unwilling to take yet another hammering. Barnato prodded him into action. He winced. Still, he stayed where he was, no longer able to register as Hammond called out impatiently, "Time!"

Barnato hoisted Francois up; he wobbled as he stood. Taking advantage of his vulnerability, Savage hit him at will. From among the assembled crowd, Rogaly jeered, shouting across at Barnato, "Throw in the sponge before your man gets killed!" Kate winced in pain and shock.

"Then, by God, he'll just have to die. No way do I give up that easily," Barnato retorted angrily.

Savage now tried unsuccessfully to set Francois up for the killer punch but succeeded only in rabbit-punching him behind the ear as Francois seemed to pull himself together. He weaved and bobbed to avoid the onslaught of punches. "I'll lay sixty-to-three on Savage! Eighty-to-three," The odds kept rising as Rogaly shouted with excitement, "One-hundred-to-three on Savage!"

Barnato responded meeting the challenge. "I'll take your last bet."

"How often?" Rogaly baited him.

"As many times as you damn well like!" Barnato roared back infuriated.

"All right. I'll lay it to you fifty times." Rogaly hooked the bait.

"It's a bet!" Barnato accepted the wager.

The end of round 17 found Francois still on his feet. Dazed, battered, cut over his left eye and bruised, he limped back to his stool, disorientated as to the time but coherent and conscious of the roar from the crowd. Nearby a digger jested snidely, "Wonder if Kate's been sleeping around? Bet he can't even put it away there!"

The rough crowd hooted their approval. Kate blushed with shame. She wanted to stand up for herself and defend Francois at the same time, but she stood tongue-tide in front of so many men. *What would Francois do about it! What could he do?*

From within the stunned recesses of his mind, Francois heard and understood the insult. No one was going to talk about his Kate that way.

From across the ring, Savage put in his pennyworth. "He's so bad, he can't even be used for stud purposes!" Again, the crowd roared with laughter. Kate covered her face.

Suddenly, Francois reacted. He raised his head in a fit of anger. "What the hell did you say?" Rage boiled inside him. He rushed from his stool and caught Savage with a flurry of punches straight to the face as Hammond quickly sounded the gong.

Francois' attack culminated in a looping right uppercut which knocked Savage senseless to the ground. Kneeling, Francois passed his left arm beneath Savage's armpits and continued smashing him in the face with his right.

Barnato screamed across the ring at Farrar, "For God's sake, throw in the sponge! Your man will be killed, and we'll all be had up for manslaughter. Give up, you fool!"

Farrar fished the sponge out of the bucket and threw it into the ring as Hammond tried desperately to pull Francois off Savage. He seemed to have worked off his anger and came away without too much protest.

Immediately, Farrar and Phillips rushed into the ring and carried the unconscious boxer away while jubilant diggers thronged around Francois and Barnato. They slapped him on the back as he stared trance-like at them. He was a winner, unaware of some hidden force that had driven him beyond his depleted reserves of strength. At last, he had shown them just what calibre of man he was.

Barnato whooped with delight as the pounds started rolling in. He loved making a profit.

Kate flushed with pride at the man who had defended her honour. Now she knew what he had never managed to tell her—that he really cared.

It was a beautiful morning with dew on the ground as Josh and Joseph prepared to leave with Oom Hendrik and his family. Somewhat amused, the old warrior turned to Josh.

"Kleinbaas got a hole in his nose for the ring?" he joked as he watched Josh staring at Karina. Giggling, he avoided Josh's affectionate slap.

"Kleinbaas want a little water to put out the fire in his belly?"

"If you don't stop that nonsense, you old bugger, I'll have to leave you behind," Josh teased.

"Sorry, Kleinbaas." His white teeth gleamed in his ebony face. "I was remembering some of my wives from a long time ago."

"You too old to do anything else now, you old lion." Josh laughed.

Grinning as they mounted their horses, they both turned and waved to those left behind. Kate stood between Pisani and a still swollen, bandaged Francois.

Boer farmers had a hard and isolated life. Typically, the farmhouse consisted of a long living room, a kitchen and two or three bedrooms for the family of maybe as many as eleven. A stable housed the horse and cows, and the outbuildings also had a hayloft and straw for the chickens and domestic animals.

During summer months, berries grew wild in the bush, and all jams were made of strawberry, raspberry, and others. Mushrooms were plentiful after the rains. They usually had a cellar, and in summer the fresh meat and all milk products were kept in there.

During the winter big barrels of pickled cucumbers, sour cabbage, and beetroot were prepared. Apples and pears were kept in the loft in layers of straw, and goose fat was very popular. All those provisions had to last over the winter months as there were no fresh vegetables or fruit.

Once a month there was a fair at the nearest small *dorp* where the farmers brought their goods to sell. Tents would go up, and all sorts of things were sold, such as eggs, poultry, skins, hides, pigs' hair for brushes, ducks, and geese. Horses were sold, and with the money they earned, the Boers could buy luxuries from other traders such as sugar, salt, flour, candles, paraffin. Of course, there was also the *boeremusiek* and beer houses.

Sunday morning the church bells rang, shops and beer houses closed, and everyone put on their best clothes. The women wore snow-white starched headscarves, which came to a point and fastened under their chin.

They also used to close up the windows for the cold not to penetrate. The window frames were sealed with newspapers, and the sills were covered in cotton wool and then decorated with coloured paper.

The self-cooker was always on the go, and they usually drank black tea. Tea was drunk in glasses, only coffee or milk tea was drunk in cups, and they were used to make her own wine. The mead was made with hops and left to ferment, and when the corks were opened, it used to shoot out. Everyone had a particular job.

In summer they all went to bathe in the river. Separate places were allotted to men and women, and the youngsters who went to the river in crowds, bathed naked, with fun and laughter ringing all over the fields.

Hendrik, his wife Tienie, Mariana, Karina and Josh sat around the dinner table as the patriarch closed his Bible, having just finished a thanksgiving prayer. Tienie and the girls cleared the table while Hendrik poured himself a drink.

Josh stole another glance at Karina as the women folk returned to the table. Sipping his drink thoughtfully, Hendrik eyed first his daughter and then Josh. A smile curled around his weather-beaten face as he looked across at his wife. "Mama, where did I put that candle? You know, that half-inch stump I was having to get Karina married with?"

Tienie returned his wink with abroad grin that lit up her plump rosy face. "Oh, I threw it away, I'm so sorry!" They both turned to face an alarmed Josh and Karina as Hendrik continued.

"Mama, then Josh won't be able to talk to Karina." He smiled. "No candle, no chatter."

Karina's face dropped.

Smiling, Hendrik withdrew the candle he had silently secreted in his pocket. "Mama, do you think this is too long a piece for them?"

"Far too long," Tienie replied teasingly as Karina looked furious. "Hendrik, look at the boy, he'll fall fast asleep before it's half-burnt."

After stealing another look at the disappointment etched on the young people's faces, she lit the candle and took Hendrik's arm. They left the room. Mariana, however, remained and drew out her sewing basket.

"I've got so much mending to do. I think I'll sit here with you and do it." Beaming at them, she lifted the lid.

"Come on, Mariana!" Karina glowered at her. "Can't you see we want to be alone?"

Her eyes flickered over Josh. He was looking at Karina like some lovesick fool. Suddenly there was no place for a third person here. "Oh, all right," Mariana relented. "I'll go now."

Pale, white light crept through the room as the evening sky gave way to the gathering darkness. The room was filled with a warm glow. Coyly, Karina approached Josh. Slowly their lips touched.

CHAPTER 8

Johannesburg
Capitalist cold and callous,
Destitute of love and hate
Furnished arms to homeless vagrants
To deluge with blood the state.

In Johannesburg, the Uitlander dissatisfaction with nepotism and corruption of officials persisted. What upset them most was that the prices and quality of essential goods for the mining industry were adversely affected by the government's system of concessions. This included the supply of water to Johannesburg, manufacture and distribution of liquor and dynamite, and the construction of railway lines.

Taking another sip from his drink, Farrar turned the page of the newspaper and read on. Next to him, Barnato, Phillips and Francois chatted amiably as members of the Johannesburg Club passed to and fro nodding an occasional greeting.

The rustling of paper caused the threesome to glance up at Farrar. "Have you read the leading article today?" he asked, once having gained their attention. "It's good stuff. Just what's wanted." He pushed the newspaper across the table. "You're the educated one, Lionel, read it out for the others."

Skimming through the article, Phillips came to an abrupt halt. "Here's a good bit. Listen. 'Johannesburg has nothing it requires to make it fairly habitable or ordinarily safe and healthy. The attempt to make it so by self-taxation and local control is denied. Nothing remains at present but to await the issue of the promises made by the President. If they aren't satisfactory, a stronger, more continual and louder demand must be made for that which is universally granted in other civilised communities.'"

"Not bad, hey?" Phillips looked satisfied. "It's about time they listened to our needs!"

"Sanitation isn't the only thing," Farrar growled. "The place is getting more difficult to live in, despite the fact that we, the diggers, have made it into one of the most flourishing cities in the world!"

"Who's booming?" Barnato objected as he set his drink down. "Have you seen the latest prices? I'll tell you who's making a fat profit. The government! They just about doubled every official's salary in the short time we've been here!"

"I hear," Francois butted in, "Old Kruger is very annoyed at all these suggestions that we doubt his word or that he's broken his promise."

"For God's sake!" Barnato was exasperated. He whipped his steel-rimmed glasses from the bridge of his nose. "We wouldn't doubt his word if he'd done anything about it! Does he think we're a bunch of schoolboys to be scolded when he's cross with us? Or that we can be bought off with a lollipop when we ask to be allowed to run our own lives and our businesses? What about the railway line he's been promising us for years?"

The group lapsed into momentary silence as they contemplated Barnato's angry outburst.

"What are the chances in the Volksraad?" Phillips asked.

"Not a hope," Francois replied with a shake of the head. "This is the way

Kruger wants it and precisely how he'll keep it. With a few exceptions, he's got the *Raad* behind him." He sighed. "They'd do without the railways altogether if they had their way. They reckon that as it's only you Uitlanders that'll get any benefit from them, you should do all the necessary paying. Broadly speaking, that's his attitude to almost everything on the mines including dynamite."

Barnato cradled his chin in his palm of his hand. His elbow rested on the arm of his chair as he became pensive. "You know," he commented, "a lot of our troubles would disappear if old Kruger could be persuaded to retire and let some of the liberals in. He won't take heed of public opinion, he never reads the newspaper, let alone take any advice from the more visionary men around him. People like General Joubert or Louis Botha, for instance."

Hammond suddenly burst into the room. "Have you heard?" angrily waving a copy of *The Standard*. He grabbed the bottle and poured himself a stiff measure. "Bill Brown of *The Standard* was arrested early this morning!"

For a moment, the scene froze as glasses hung in mid-air between counter and lip; words stopped in mid-sentence. The cloth in the busy hands of the barman came to a dead stop in a puddle of beer, while the amber liquid from the bottle of scotch poured by Barnato into his glass seemed to suspend its flow. Then the baffled chorus of questions began as Hammond held up his hand like a judge demanding silence.

"He was arrested for *lese-majesty*," Hammond explained.

"Treason against the king," Barnato exclaimed angrily. "But we don't even live under royal rule in the Transvaal!"

"You remember that article in *The Standard* last month?" remarked Phillips. "I think it was entitled 'Reform or Revolution'. That's what did it!"

"I thought there'd be trouble," Francois put in. "With all due respect, it seems the Johannesburg papers forget they're published in an independent republic, not part of the British Empire."

"We're getting away from the subject," Phillips interrupted. "What about Bill Brown? Where is he now? They haven't put him in the Pretoria jail, have they?"

"No, he's out on his own recognisance," Hammond replied as he drank thirstily. "I believe he's publishing a denial to the charges in tomorrow's paper. Claims they're untrue and unfounded, and the article contained nothing that could cause sedition or high treason. So, we'd better keep our opinions to ourselves."

"Hear, hear," echoed the others.

"I think it would be wiser, as this matter can now be considered *sub judice* if we refrain from further comment." Phillips added, rising and surveying the others. "You never know who's listening these days. Let's wait and see what happens at the meeting tonight."

Diggers crowded into the club as the day gave way to a clear, warm, starlit evening. They all knew the reason for their presence. An air of suppressed rage was evident among the assembled men. This anger snowballed after they found out that someone had ripped down the notices advertising the meeting. Was this an attempt to sabotage the gathering?

Kate glanced expectantly at Francois, seated next to her. Then her gaze fell on Farrar and Pisani sitting among some noisy diggers. On the platform, Barnato and Hammond took their seats alongside Phillips amid loud cheers.

Phillips gestured to the assembled crowd to quieten down and rose to address them. "We have now only two questions to consider. What do we want, and how shall we get it?"

We want the establishment of the republic as a true one; reduced taxation; abolishment of religious barriers; two official languages; reduction of the franchise qualifications, and free trade in South African products. That is what we're after!" Phillips shouted, shaking his fist at the crowd. He paused momentarily before retaking his seat amid their hearty applause.

Barnato adjusted his glasses on the bridge of his nose and straightened his tight, ill-fitting jacket. He rose, his hands firmly stuck inside his bulky pants pockets. Silently he gazed at the assembled crowd. A slow smile crept across his lips as he took out one hand and withdrew a fat Havana cigar.

"What made me keen on coming to speak to you chaps tonight was that I received several messages to say that if I came, I'd be shot. Well, here I am—who's got the pluck to shoot me?" He grinned again as he blew smoke into the air while the assembly roared their approval.

"I don't know what our next move must be. The government clearly thinks it has done well for the industry, and the opposition will, of course, irritate old Kruger." He waggled his forefinger. "The old man is, however, in no way friendly to the industry. He has the most perverted ideas on political economy. He suspects we are imperialists and jingoes, and that Rhodes is pulling the strings."

He paused as another wave of laughter broke forth. "What we want is a President who'll act as such, one who can understand English and certainly Dutch, and who," he emphasised before he concluded, "will be dependent at times on his friends, you and me!"

The cheers rose to a crescendo as he puffed on his glowing cigar and waved back in his peculiar style.

Hammond hesitated. His talk was to help ferment dissent among the people, as those who pulled strings, the real power brokers for whom he worked had told him to do. He half-smiled then rose to speak. His stance was aggressive.

"Who formed the Transvaal? We came here and found the original burghers settled on farms. They hadn't any market or means. We enabled them to live. Who made the markets for them? We did! Yet we're told that we're mere birds of passage, that they were here before us, and we haven't any rights."

A ripple of agreement could be heard in the crowd.

"When approached on the subject of a reduction of taxation, they reply, 'No! Dammit! These people are all rich, they can pay.' Memorandums are sent to the Volksraad and referred to a committee. They are never heard of again!" Now he rocked back and forth on his heels. "Unless we rise up as one man and give vent to our feelings, we shall never be understood or listened to. It has never yet been done, but I do hope this meeting will accomplish it!"

He sat down abruptly as the audience echoed their support. Some brandished their fists. Hats were tossed into the air. They spun, then floated down into outstretched hands. The people were ready for a change.

Their horses cantered rhythmically as Josh and Oom Hendrik topped the rise. Three yellow shapes trotted across the track a hundred yards ahead. Their bodies blended in with the veld as they ran to a safe distance. Then they stopped and stood erect, their ears cocked, their noses twitching.

Below, a river meandered slowly through the lush green valley. Reining in his horse, Oom Hendrik gazed dreamily at the surrounding countryside, his hands resting on the pommel of the leather saddle. He glanced fleetingly at Josh before returning to stare at the spectacle in front of them.

"You like it?" he snapped.

"Yes!" Josh enthused, still eyeing it.

Oom Hendrik smiled and wiped his sweaty brow with the back of his wrist. "I kept it for my son, but the good Lord has given me only daughters." He sighed as he watched the river move along. "It's a wonderful place."

"The river runs well." Josh agreed with him.

Oom Hendrik smiled wistfully, then pointed to the ribbon of water below them. "It's never once dried up. River runs like that all year round."

"It's almost better than your home farm," Josh reflected.

"Yes," the older man answered, deep in thought. "I would have settled here, but I reckoned it would be better to keep it for a son. It would give him a good start, and he'd get joy out of it."

Hendrik swung his foot out of the stirrup and dismounted. His boot left a deep solitary impression of his presence in the loose, fertile soil. Josh followed suit as Hendrik settled himself against the trunk of an overhanging willow tree. His legs were outstretched as he passed a soiled handkerchief over his moist brow. He removed his hat as Josh settled down beside him and continued to gaze down at the winding river snaking through the green valley below.

"When a man has a fine farm and many cattle, it is a great sorrow for him not to have a son. The continuance of the family is interrupted. My daughters will only bear the promises of other men." He filled his pipe with tobacco, lit it and inhaled deeply so that the tobacco glowed dull orange. He slowly exhaled.

"You know, boy, I like you very much. I have wondered why it is that I have no sons, for my father had some, and they all have male heirs, but I have none. Then I thought of my wife's family. Five girls and they all had daughters. So, you see my boy, where the trouble is. It's on that side." He sighed, "That's where the girl seed is. Now, Karina is like her mother was; slender, dark, with a spirit that was—" He searched for the words suddenly lost in memory. Now a joyous smile slowly creased his jaw. "Like that horse of yours. Spirited and lively." He turned his gaze full on Josh.

"Now the other girl, Mariana, she's just like my mother. Spitting image of her. You see my boy, on one side, the girl seed, on the other, the seed that makes sons. This land and 100 head of cattle go as a dowry with Mariana. The man who marries her gets the land." He pointed down the valley drawing on his pipe again and relaxed back against the tree trunk.

Josh's mouth hung agape. He was stunned.

"And with Karina?" he stammered.

"*Ag*, a few odds and ends. She is her own dowry. The man who marries her gets a beauty." He sucked on his pipe, looked pensive and said no more.

Josh sat rigid, trying to suppress his mounting anxiety. Confused, he shook his head. "I don't know what to say, Oom."

"Then say nothing," Hendrik replied. He took a last draw on his pipe as he gathered up his hat. "You will not marry for three years unless you want to make the contract now. We can always make a private arrangement, hey."

Josh remained silent as Hendrik paused, waiting for a reply. He nudged the youngster gently.

"It will all take time and plenty of talk between the parties and the parents." He smiled and made his way towards the horses who were grazing peacefully nearby. He paused, hand outstretched over the saddle, and turned to face Josh. "I just wanted you to know, so we can deal openly and honestly with each other."

After the ride back, they unbuckled their saddles in front of the farmyard. Oom Hendrik lifted his on to his shoulder and made his way to the barn. Josh dawdled deliberately until Joseph emerged from its interior. He went up to his friend and confidant and spilt out all the confusion that filled his heart and mind.

"What do you think I must do?"

Joseph looked down at the young slip of a lad who was weighed down with problems. Even his shoulders drooped. "*Aikona.*" He smiled. "*Kleinbaas*, how long does a man lie in bed with his eyes open and a pretty wife to look at?"

"How should I know?" Josh was puzzled.

Joseph stared back at him with a kind but earthy expression. "How long does a man work on his lands and with his cattle?"

Slowly the penny dropped. Josh shook his head vigorously, for his heart was ruled by love, not logic. "No, Joseph, that wouldn't be right."

"All I say is that Kleinbaas has got dreams in his head. Women are not dreams. They are made for a man's comfort." He patted the lad of his shoulder. "Sometimes a man has a soft bed, but he doesn't live there."

The wax ran down the sides of the candle, giving off an eerie glow as it formed moulded sculptures of solid stalactites before it reached the table. Neither Josh nor Karina noticed the shapes in the flickering glow of the partially lit room.

"So, that's what your pa told, honest." Josh hadn't left out a single detail.

Karina felt her arms and the upper part of her body go limp. Her small breasts rested on the table as she breathed with a choked feeling. She stared back at Josh, stung by what he had told her. Slowly the hurt expression gave way to one of fiery anger as her hazel eyes flashed. "My pa wouldn't deceive us like that! He wouldn't!"

"Well, he has," Josh stated. "And he's not going to change his mind, either, Karina."

She spoke quickly. "You're going to take me away into the veld before dawn! I'll slip into my room now and pack. I'm finished with my ma and pa!" Her face was flushed, and tears trickled from her eyes. "To say that I'm incapable of producing sons. How dare they?" Her face became daring and full of challenge. "If you're a man, you will take me now!" She unbuttoned her blouse, stood up and moved closer to him.

Josh broke out in a sweat as an uncomfortable feeling spread over him. He had never anticipated it would come to this. He *liked* Karina, maybe even loved her – but he didn't *want* her, and couldn't *marry* her; not yet, anyway. He was still far too young to consider such a step. He struggled for a reply and the words caught in his throat. "Don't be silly," he stammered.

Karina looked at him, her mouth agape. She shook her head as tears welled up. "You must. Please. I want you, my love."

Josh stood up, confused and uncertain. "Let's wait and see. We'll make a plan. Tomorrow's another day." He left the room quickly and made his way down the dark silent corridor.

Josh contemplated the day's events as he lay stretched out on his bed. Suddenly the door creaked open. He sat up, startled.

Karina saw his expression of surprise as she came closer and lifted her nightgown. She no longer cared about the shame of what she was doing. She'd show them that she was capable of producing sons! Then Josh would never be able to leave her. She slipped her nightgown over her head and let it fall to the floor, revealing her naked body of slender proportions. Standing there, an impish smile playing around her lips.

Josh swallowed hard. She smiled without a hint of uncertainty. *I'll show them all*, she thought as she pulled back the bedcovers and got in next to him.

Josh started to sweat at the closeness of her warmth and beauty. He remained still. A new, uneasy feeling was penetrating his body – especially the lower part.

"For God's sake, Karina," he whispered, frightened.

"You don't love me." She pouted as she took his clammy hand and held it against her firm breast. Her taut nipple protruded between his fingers.

Josh looked anxiously into her lovely face. "I do love you, Karina, but hell, I won't be alive to love you if your pa comes in." He did not respond to her caresses.

"You're not a man!" She glared at him. How could he resist her fingers which now undid his pyjama buttons and trailed along his hairless chest?

"Hell, of course, I am," He retorted, firmly, encouraged by the desire which her touch evoked.

"Then prove it," she demanded and untied the cord of his pyjama pants. Her hand groped for him.

The sensation was overpowering as Karina continued to explore, her shiny black hair warm against his hot, sweaty face. Josh found that he was breathing in gulps as his heart pounded, and wild thoughts flew through his head. *But Kate, you never explained how persuasive a woman can be.*

She kissed him again as she rolled her sensuous body over his. Her breathing increased as she guided his hand from her breast to the hub of her warmth, her soft moistening folds. With a supreme effort, Josh rolled away, pushing her from him.

Karina slid out of bed on to the cold floor in an ungainly heap. She stood up angrily, her dignity dented as she grabbed her nightgown.

Pulling it on, she turned with her head held high and stormed out of the room, slamming the door behind her.

"The girl needs a beating," Oom Hendrik remarked as Josh and Joseph saddled their horses. Dawn had just broken as the Strydom girls stood silently close to their mother. "Perhaps it won't be necessary to tell your father everything." Hendrik continued. "A man has many a shame when he has nothing but daughters! Perhaps you won't want to add to them by saying that he cannot control them." His thick Dutch accent was choked with emotion, and his face wore an imploring look. Josh felt sorry for him, even though the wily old Afrikaner had tried to trick him.

"I'll say nothing, Oom Hendrik, except that I enjoyed my little holiday and that much could happen in three or four years."

Hendrik studied the lad. He somehow seemed more mature than he had been the day before. "That will be a kindness, my boy. Perhaps you'll think a little about the land and the cattle you have seen?"

Josh nodded. "I will, Oom."

Hendrik smiled uncertainly. "Maybe you'll ride this way again?"

"That might also be," Josh answered.

"I'm truly sorry, my boy, but you see what a cross is laid on a man when he has no sons. You would not, I'm sure, wish to bear such a burden yourself." He smiled again and stretched out his hand. Josh clasped it firmly then stepped back as Karina approached coyly. They gazed hesitantly at each other, then she kissed him gently on the cheek.

Josh smiled as he mounted his horse. He turned once more and faced the Strydoms, giving them a farewell wave. Then he dug his knee into his horse's rib and rode off alongside Joseph. A feeling of freedom and adventure gripped him once more as the wind whistled through his hair. His flaxen locks flapped rhythmically behind him.

Joseph hummed his friend, Enoch Sontonga's new catchy hymn, *Nkosi Sikelel iAfrika*, and then chuckled as Josh rode past him. "Hey, Kleinbaas, hold it in! Keep it for a nice filly, a nut-brown, or a white one. Maybe we meet one along the road." Still chuckling, "Lots of hot young fillies in the world."

"Only the horse kind will be for me for a long time," Josh retorted, then grinned sheepishly. The two men both laughed out loud.

CHAPTER 9

There were several financial houses dominated by Cecil John Rhodes, as well as other large businesses in budding Johannesburg, controlled and run by the likes of Alfred Beit, Barney Barnato, Hermann Eckstein, Abe Bailey, Joseph Benjamin Robinson, George Farrar and Lionel Phillips.

The grievances of the Uitlanders, largely excluded from the vote, provided both cause and cover for a conspiracy between British officials, the Cape Colony's Prime Minister Cecil Rhodes, and mining capitalists. The time was ripe for rebellion.

These immigrants formed a Reform Committee with Percy FitzPatrick as the secretary and led by Colonel Frank Rhodes (brother of Cecil), Hammond (Rhodes' employee), Phillips, Farrar and others, with the aim of bringing pressure to bear on Kruger to meet their demands.

These Randlords were banging heads with Kruger's government, principally over the high taxes demanded from them, the dynamite monopoly owned by the government, and the insistence that Afrikaans be the first language in schools. Also, of course, the absence of the franchise for the Uitlanders. The government under President Paul Kruger had made promises but failed to keep them.

Meanwhile, Kruger was aware that trouble was brewing in Johannesburg and that, behind the scenes of the internal conflict within the Transvaal, a larger issue was at stake, that of British supremacy as against republican independence. He felt that the matter of the extension of the franchise to the newcomers was merely being used as a cat's-paw to further the Rhodes' schemes. However, he did confer burgher rights on all Uitlanders who served in Transvaal commandos.

Kruger dismissed all such petitions, asserting that enfranchising "these newcomers, these disobedient persons" might imperil the republic's independence. "Protest!" he shouted at one Uitlander deputation. "What is the use of protesting? I have the guns, you haven't".

Under these circumstances, Jo'burg became increasingly tense. Business along the whole of the Rand ground to a halt, with traders and their families anxious to leave town.

The government, however, was uncomfortably aware that many of the foreigners' grievances were only too real. Kruger was unusually conciliatory and made some efforts to soften some of the regulations and taxes, such that the tension was eased. People started to go about their business.

It was a sultry morning with an early promise of afternoon thunderstorms as crowds began to gather expectantly in the Market Square. Below the balcony, a banner advertising the President's visit was flanked by *vierkleur* flags of the South African Republic which fluttered in the breeze.

Inside the stone building, a welcoming committee, including du Plessis, Farrar, Hammond and Phillips milled around the President. Swarthy and soberly dressed with a black top hat sitting firmly on his head, the President's beard was white and full. A stern expression was fixed on his face, and his eyes looked cold. His black jacket was ill-fitting and tight around his portly midriff.

"Just be careful of your words while in this town," He was advised by Francois. "Remember, you're among the wolves."

"This is neither the time nor the place for an argument, Mynheer du

Plessis," Kruger glared at him. "I'm glad that I came here. Thank you for your welcome." He glanced at the others and nodded in appreciation. "I wanted to come and hear for myself all about Johannesburg. For that reason, I organised this meeting, after which I will meet your deputation representing Johannesburg so that we may go more deeply into these matters." He turned and made his way out onto the balcony. The others followed dutifully.

Kate watched from below as the familiar beaver frockcoat and blue-green sash appeared on the balcony amid a few scattered cheers drowned by intermittent booing. A stony, silent air of tolerance prevailed among the majority of the assembled crowd.

Kruger gazed down at them, these people from the outside world from whom he and his fellow burghers had trekked in their covered wagons. They had moved far inland, over mountains, forging rivers, cutting a path, and fighting the sleeping sickness, and the black tribes. They had trailed far into the deserted, wild interior of Africa, finally stopping to cultivate the land and rear their cattle in peace. Now his people had to tolerate these fortune hunters who once again threatened their existence and that of their republic. Should he try to appease them?

He shook his head sadly and grimaced. Taking a large handkerchief from his pocket, he blew his nose with a loud, trumpeting sound. Then for a moment or two, he loomed large above them, filling the silence with his bulk and hostility.

"People of the Lord, you old burghers, you foreigners, newcomers, yes, even you thieves and murderers!" Kruger began addressing them in the foreign, hated language, English.

Before he could continue, Rogaly interrupted by shouting at his fellow diggers. His shock of carrot-coloured hair gleamed in the sun. "Now we know what the old devil thinks of us!"

The crowd bawled its agreement as many tongues were loosened by the fiery Irishman. Kate caught up in the enthusiasm of the congregation, raised her fist in unison with the crowd. "Rule Britannia," echoed through the square.

Kruger became even more formidable as he jabbed his finger at the crowd. "*Bly stil!*", he commanded, raising his gruff voice. "You outsiders must keep silent if you wish to hear me speak."

He paused, waiting for the babble to subside. "As you are aware, I have laboured with difficulties in getting the railway from Lourenco Marques into the interior of this country."

"For us, the people, you call outsiders?" Rogaly shouted. "We're as good as you are. And better! You treat us with contempt." A mixture of cheers, laughter and boos emanated from the assembled diggers as Kruger paled.

"Bly stil!" he shouted again and then carried on in a gruff manner. "I have no scorn for the new population, only for men such as you!"

The colour returned to his cheeks as he continued. "I am bound on a mission to our brothers and neighbours in the Orange Free State to advocate both a railway connection and the Union of South Africa. This is not to be accomplished to the detriment of any one state, but in the interests and welfare of the whole land." He paused, waiting for applause, but there was only a hushed silence.

"And what about us?" Kate shouted, breaking the stillness. Francois, who saw her from above, shifted his weight uneasily.

"Yes, what about the Cape Railway? And the line from Natal? Is it because they operated by the British?" Rogaly shouted, his Irish blood flowing fast.

"As to the franchise question," Kruger rambled on. "I will not discriminate in my treatment of old and new burghers, except on one or two points, namely in regard to voting and representation in the

Volksraad. But I will endeavour as far as possible to meet your wishes in those matters."

"We want our rights! Taxes must fall! We demand the vote!" Rogaly screamed. His fist was clenched as booing erupted from sections of the crowd.

"The Uitlanders are not good enough to vote, and yet we must not only pay the government taxes but fight for them too!" Kate shouted as her heart pounded with excitement. *Why shouldn't she be part of the action too?* The crowd became disorderly as calls for justice rang out.

Seething with rage at this disrespectful scene, Kruger gripped the balcony railing. His knuckles whitened as he struggled to control his temper. Sensing his anger, the diggers quietened down.

The antagonisers and the antagonised faced each other in silence. Kruger glared at them ominously but with great authority before he addressed them again.

"I cannot say I am quite satisfied insofar as there is a section of this community here who are inclined to overstep the boundaries of the law."

The group behind him glanced uneasily about.

"I have my spies here. I know who of you are loyal to the government and those who are my sworn enemies. Should any trouble arise, I shall call the law-abiding diggers to settle this matter themselves. But if this should not prove satisfactory, I will be compelled to call up the burghers. Then I will have to call those diggers, 'rebels' and deal with them accordingly."

A low, rebellious murmur filtered through the crowd as the President's words sank in. Behind him, the group stared in astonishment as he continued. "I shall now retire to meet the deputation." Saying this, he turned his back on the crowd, rammed his black top hat back on his head and stormed off the balcony. His followers trailed behind him.

Rogaly took advantage of the stunned, still seething crowd as he jumped up onto a wooden fruit box. "Are we going to stand for this?" he demanded.

The crowd hesitated.

"To hell with Kruger," Rogaly bellowed. "We haven't finished with him yet. We've still got a few messages for him to take back to Pretoria. But how can we give them to him when we don't know where the bastard's got to?"

A voice rang out, "He's gone to the Government Building!"

Fists clenched, Rogaly gazed around at the expectant looks on the diggers' faces. Then he punched the air. "Well, then, what are we waiting for? We'll follow him to the Government Building!"

The crowd started to move noisily en masse down the road.

Inside, the office was comfortably furnished with luxurious dark leather and oak chairs in browns. The satin complemented the oval, well-polished, heavy stinkwood table around which Francois, Farrar, Hammond, and Phillips, among others, faced the President. They listened cautiously to what he was saying.

"You want me to withdraw some duties and then ask for large sums of money!" Kruger gazed slowly from face to face with hate-filled eyes. "Taxes must be removed, you say, and more money spent on public works? The new Government Building here, off Market Square, costs more than 300,000 pounds! There are all your roads and lighting. The Sanitary Board never stops asking me for money. Where is it all to come from if you don't pay taxes?" He sat back in the chair, the leather creaking. He lifted his pipe out of the ashtray and, slowly puffing, relit it. All the while, he watched and sized up the delegation.

Hammond spoke first, respectfully addressing the President. His

American drawl at first caused Kruger some difficulty.

"It's hardly fair, Your Honour, that the present inhabitants should bear the whole burden of costs for roads and buildings that will be used by many future generations." He gazed around the room for support from his colleagues, but all he could hear was the echo of distant jeering.

The President removed his pipe, coughed and replied. "The succeeding generations will have enough to pay for on their own account, Mynheer Hammond." The chanting of the diggers wafted through the wide-open windows behind Kruger. "What is that noise?" he demanded, looking around the group.

The men shifted nervously, attempting to hide their discomfort as the chanting grew louder. Their gaze fell on Phillips, maybe because he was the oldest and most respected. Their reticence increased with the President's annoyance as he withdrew the pipe from his mouth with one angry motion.

Phillips rose, trying to think of an answer that would satisfy Kruger as the din from the crowd increased. "It's only the crowd in the Market Square celebrating Your Honour's presence in the Transvaal. Is there anything you can add, Mr President, to what you said about railways?" quickly changing the subject as he retook his seat.

Again, the crowd jeered as the volume of their displeasure grew, as the men singing British patriotic songs, tore down and trampled on the vierkleur flag.

"We want Kruger! Go fetch him."

Inside the room, the atmosphere grew tense, all eyes converged on the most sought-after man in the town.

The heavy entrance oak door creaked open and the crowd hushed expectantly. Furious, Francois emerged, glaring at the unruly mob.

"The President will receive one of your numbers to hear your complaints."

The crowd surged forward, unanimously supporting Rogaly, and pushed him towards the doorway. Cheers of encouragement echoed about him.

"Take that drunk out of here! I will not hear what he has to say!" Kruger shouted when he recognised the heckler.

"You listen to me, Paul Kruger!" Rogaly barked arrogantly, refusing to budge. "Do you know that you're insulting the people of Johannesburg?"

"No, I didn't know that," Kruger responded, his eyes flaming. "But I do know that I am insulting you. *Voetsak!*"

Rogaly had no choice but to leave; he was surrounded by a solid flank of Kruger supporters. He emerged outside in front of the expectant crowd. In a fury he addressed them. "They kicked me out. And he told me to voetsak, like a dog! It's an insult to the whole town! Are we going to let those bloody Dutchmen treat us this way?"

Angry cries greeted him in unison. "No! No! Shame!" Then they broke out in spontaneous singing. "For he's a jolly good fellow," then "Rule Britannia, Britannia rules the waves".

Suddenly the singing stopped. The mood changed. "We want Kruger! Bring him out!" Their cries swelled the air as they surged forward menacingly towards the oak door.

Instantly the door opened as Francois' bulk framed the doorway, rifle in hand, and levelled in the direction of the nearest group of figures, then the entire mob. "I'll shoot any man who comes a step nearer!"

His eyes met Kate's as he caught sight of her. Her lips tightly clenched as she stood proudly among the group at the forefront of the mob. She stared back at him, turned suddenly and pushed her way back through the crowd, as the front ranks edged forward by those at the rear, pressed backwards.

Suddenly, a few bricks and a stick sailed through the air as a digger lunged at a flagpole. Raising his rifle again, Francois swung around, aiming it at him, and he hesitated in his tracks.

"If you touch that rope, I'll shoot you!" Francois threatened coldly. He ducked as a brick sailed through the air, missing him by a hair's breadth. Raising his rifle above the crowd, Francois fired. The effect was immediate, as deafened by the noise, the mob grew silent. Francois lowered his arm and directed the firearm at them. Wispy smoke curled upward from its muzzle as behind him policemen rushed from their station brandishing their carbines in the direction of the mob.

Fists were raised in defiance. Cries of "God save the Queen!" echoed as they began breaking up and moving off down the road in angry groups.

Francois watched for some moments, then heaved a sigh of relief before turning and re-entering the building.

"Do you know who those people remind me of, du Plessis?" Kruger gestured as he walked up to him. "An old baboon chained up in my yard. I have had this animal for a long time, and we're good friends. While feeding it the other day, I caught its tail by accident in the fence. Immediately, it jumped at me and bit me on the hand. Me, the one that had just been giving it food. Tomorrow, du Plessis, you can tell your Uitlander friends that even if they aren't baboons, they sometimes behave like them. And you can also let them know that I'll never set foot in Johannesburg again!"

Tall gum trees with strips of peeling bark grew alongside the banks of the stream. The small flowers of the gum tree attracted bees, resulting in a steady hum as the insects collected nectar. Nearby the leafy branches fluttered in the warm evening breeze. Joseph listened, captivated, his wooden knobkerrie on the ground next to him as Josh read aloud from his Bible.

A stump-tail lizard came from under the tree's roots and lay absorbing the sun's last rays, its flat head levelled in their direction. High above them in the sky, a wedge-tailed eagle hung suspended, searching the earth below for prey.

Puzzled, Joseph interrupted as a fly crawled up his bare brown back. "All the Earth is the Lord's and all the things thereof. The white men are afraid of him, but the Induna does not fear anything, only respect. He must be a great chief to make the white people frightened of his command and keep them in fear without ever coming among them to make an example."

"But the Lord is a spirit, Joseph," Josh explained innocently.

"Really," Joseph retorted in disbelief.

"No, truly he is," Josh persisted.

Joseph smiled, "Kleinbaas, read me the story of Gideon." He sat back against the tree trunk and listened intently.

"In the battle of Gideon against the Midianite, the Lord said to Gideon; The people that go with you are too many to give the Midianites into their hands lest Israel vaunts itself against me saying, 'Our hands have saved us.' So, Gideon had to reduce his army."

"*Hau*, no, don't be a fool," Joseph interrupted. Absorbed with the story, he was alarmed by its possible consequences.

Josh continued. "And when all the people of the east lay along in the valley like grasshoppers for a multitude."

"*Ai*, that's good." Joseph nodded in agreement, identifying with the continuing saga.

Gruff voices interrupted their concentration as they both held their breath and listened silently.

"Who's that?" Joseph whispered puzzled.

"Hush!" Josh tried to listen to the voices, which were becoming more audible.

"Du Plessis's place is down there," they heard Savage's voice boom through the silence. "You know what to do when you get there. Go around the back, mate. I'll throw the paraffin upfront, then we'll all just sit back and watch du Plessis fry in hell!" His mocking laugh rang loud. He imagined the fiery prospect, as they trampled through the bush.

"Ha, ha! I'd like that!" Savage's companion Greg laughed and spat the chewed tobacco through his split yellowing teeth. "That's the best place for that bastard."

"Then, as his claim will belong to nobody, we'll just move in and jump it!" Savage smirked as he rubbed his large hands together in gleeful anticipation.

"Yeah," Greg remarked. "It's like killing two birds with one stone." Now their laughter rang even louder as they pressed on.

Josh and Joseph remained motionless, camouflaged by the bushy foliage. Silently, they stared at each other. The two plotters, oblivious to their presence passed nearby, still chuckling to themselves.

"They are no good," Joseph whispered anxiously. "What do we do to stop them?"

His young friend's mind cleared as the situation resolved itself into a plan of action. "You go back and warn *Baas* Francois. I'll try and delay them."

Joseph moved swiftly off in the direction of the shack, running low; then he slowed his pace and hugged the leafy undergrowth. In the meantime, Josh attempted to head Savage off.

Hearing a noise behind them, Savage and Greg spun around, almost bumping into Josh as he ran towards them.

"Oh, I'm sorry," Josh panted.

"Whoa, boy, where are you off to?" Savage caught hold of his arm.

Josh smelt Savage's whisky-laden breath. He stared back defiantly at his captor. "Oh, I'm sorry. I didn't see you."

"What are you doing here, boy?" Savage asked gruffly, still holding his arm.

"I'm on my way to visit Oom Francois. What are you doing on his claim?" It was Josh's turn to be rude.

"Francois? You mean du Plessis?" exclaimed Savage, wide-eyed with suspicion.

"Yes, what are you doing here, Savage?" Josh asked boldly, feet apart.

"Don't get cocky with me, kid," Savage hissed menacingly.

"Watch it, mister!" Josh tried to ignore the tremble in his legs.

"Don't talk to me like that, squirt!" growled Savage angrily grabbing Josh. He brought his fist upward into the side of Josh's face. A bone-jarring smack sent Josh sprawling on to the ground, unconscious. Greg grabbed at Savage's fist as he hovered over Josh. "Leave the kid, we've got more important things to do."

Inside the shack, Kate stopped stroking the fire and sampled the guinea fowl. She added a pinch of salt. *Still bloody tough.* "I know it's silly to think as I do, that out here where you must kill to live, I feel sorry for the living things that are so harmless. Some people might do us harm, but take this bird here, it was completely innocent."

"So, you don't mind killing people," Francois chided. "Would you like me to go on a manhunt next time and bring back a man joint?" He glanced at Barnato and shook his head, "Women!"

Kate waved her fork at him. "Silly man, you know what I mean."

Outside, Joseph continued to run as fast as his tired old legs could move. He leapt over the small stream, then on through the bush. At last, he spied the smoke coming from the chimney. After sprinting the last few yards, he banged loudly on the door, shouting urgently, "Baas Francois! Joseph here!"

Francois glanced from Barnato to Kate as he put down his fork. Opening the door, he found himself gazing into the agitated eyes of his trusted old friend.

"What's wrong, Joseph?"

"Men coming here," He panted. "Want to burn down this house! Kill you! Kleinbaas Josh is trying to stop them!"

"Which direction are they coming from?" Francois asked, suddenly alert.

Joseph pointed towards the bush. "That way."

Francois hurriedly grabbed his rifle and inserted a round of bullets into the breach. He beckoned to the others to follow, then stepped out through the back door.

As Savage approached the shack cautiously, the smoky entrails of the fire wisped up skyward. Everything appeared quiet and normal. Silently, Savage trailed the paraffin around the wooden front porch as Greg crept around the rear. Striking the flint, Savage ignited the paraffin, sending up a whoosh of flames which snarled and crackled as they ate through the timber.

In triumphant delight, Savage shouted, "Du Plessis! This is Mel Savage!" A smile played around the corners of his mouth. "You have two choices, mate; either you can come out and be shot, or you can stay inside and roast. Ha, ha, ha."

The laughter rang clearly through the sound of fire devouring timber.

Edging through the bush, Francois hesitated as Savage gleefully aimed his rifle at the burning doorway. Then he moved swiftly up behind Savage.

"Not so fast. Savage!" Francois yelled; his rifle cocked. "Get those hands up. Go on, drop that bloody gun!"

Savage spun round, surprise etched on his face. He found himself staring into the rifle's muzzle. He had no choice but to throw down his weapon.

"I was only trying to frighten you for beating me." His whole manner changed to that of one who was trying to talk himself out of trouble. "Don't shoot me sport, fair dinkum!"

Greg crept up unseen behind Francois, gun in hand. Savage watched and waited for Greg to position himself. As Greg edged nearer, he shouted, "Shoot him, Greg!"

He dived sideward as a shot rang out. Spinning around, Francois saw the smoke still billowing from Pisani's rifle as Greg crumpled to the dirt. Stunned, Savage lay staring into Greg's surprised eyes. Then he grabbed for Greg's gun, drawing it out from under him, but not before Francois fired.

Savage felt his hand explode as a searing pain tore through his right arm. His gun jerked outward. The firing pin struck the bullet as it flew from his grasp. Blood spurted from his shattered hand. The bullet whistled wide, ricocheting as it thudded into Pisani's chest. The force sent him reeling backwards. A smudge of red spread across his dirty white woollen vest. An expression of surprise and pain fixed on his face. The others rushed over to him. Savage took advantage of the shift of interest from himself to Pisani and made off into the bush.

"Pisani!" Francois shouted. His eyes reflected the concern he felt for his friend.

Pisani gazed up at them, his face pale. "Josh told me about Savage's attack. I came as soon as I could," he whispered with difficulty. Bubbles of foaming blood formed on his lips and dribbled down his chin.

"You look bad," Kate whispered in a shocked voice, kneeling down next to him. Tears welled up in her eyes. "Francois, get Francois." Pisani wheezed urgently.

"It's okay, old man, take it easy." Francois tried to disguise his concern as he knelt down beside him.

"Kate." Pisani's eyes filled with pain, "I'm not going to make it. It's too late to say I'm sorry for what wrong I've done, but won't you stay with me for now?"

She tried not to sob out loud as she cradled his head in her lap and stroked his unkempt black hair. His chest was now awash with blood.

"I'll be here just as long as it takes you to get better, you silly man," she replied, trying to smile. But how could she pretend when she was so unhappy and shocked?

Pisani gazed up at her and smiled. Now the blood trickled from his mouth. It seeped onto Kate's clothes, but she didn't seem to notice. With a supreme effort, he turned his head towards Francois. The shape above him became blurred even though he tried his best to focus. The blood that filled his mouth made it impossible for him to speak. He spat it out, intent on having his final say. "Francois, my friend." His words were almost inaudible. "Please, you and Katy, look after Josh!"

"Like he's our own." Francois nodded as he swallowed the lump in his throat before he was able to reply. Pisani looked at both of them in turn. His eyes seemed to twinkle as his voice grew stronger for a moment.

"Francois, take care of her for me." Even though death was only seconds away, Pisani was still in control. He knew he had to exact a promise from Francois before it was too late.

"I will, Pisani."

Now Francois could no longer stem the flow of tears. He held on to his friend's hand tightly. Then, Pisani became still. His tortured expression of pain became one of peace as his body slackened.

Francois felt Pisani's hand go limp. He disengaged his hand and moved Pisani's body off Kate.

"He's dead, Kate." His voice edged in sadness. "And I'm to blame. I killed him."

Kate rose to his defence. "It was an accident, Francois. You cannot blame yourself!"

"Still, how can I ever forget?" Francois' face was ashen. "I can only give him a decent burial and keep my word to him. Maybe in some way that will lessen the guilt."

Now Kate gave vent to heavy choking sobs. "He was a dear man."

"I know." Francois held her close and stroked her hair. "But now, we must find Josh."

"That poor boy." Kate cried.

"We will take care of him." Francois' voice was resolute. "After all, I promised Pisani."

The burden of guilt would pass in time. But Francois was now saddled with other duties. He would make sure he honoured his pledge to his dying friend.

CHAPTER 10

Traitors swarmed within the border,
Traitors, rich with Transvaal gold,
Leagued with foreign mercenaries,
To invade the peaceful fold.

Cecil John Rhodes had come to the Kimberley diamond fields after being sent to Cape Town by his family when he was seventeen-years-old in the hope that the climate might improve his health. Scheming, buying up all the diamonds and diggers' claims he could get his hands on, he enlarged his diamond company called De Beers. This included the farm which he bought immediately when the owner mysteriously died.

By 1876, at the age of just twenty-three, Rhodes was worth as much as £40,000, a substantial sum anywhere in the empire.

Throughout the 1870s, he and his partners continued to expand their holding in the De Beers mine and, by 1878, they owned forty claims worth £9,000. However, Rhodes was no more than a minor capitalist contender in Kimberley – a name that was hinted at but scarcely noticed. It was the exceptionally wealthy diamond buyers, men like Joseph Robinson, Alfred Beit and Jules Porges, who dominated the mining industry at the time.

Rhodes was a shortish man of just under five foot eight and looked older than his years. He wore thick-rimmed glasses, had a round face with thinning hair, a small moustache, and spoke clear but clipped

English following his return from Oxford University. He was the ultimate expansionist, as Her Majesty was delighted to hear.

By the age of thirty-seven, he was earning a tidy fortune of £300,000 a year. He took possession of the land north of the Transvaal Republic in the name of British Imperialist expansion, which he called after himself, *Rhodesia*.

Rhodes now set his sights more actively on the Transvaal Boer Republic and its gold, the third-largest supply in the world. He was encouraged and advised by the British Colonial Secretary, Joseph Chamberlain, the force behind Rhodes.

Behind the scenes, Rhodes encouraged his employee, John Hays Hammond, and his brother Frank Rhodes to form an Uitlander Reform Committee to agitate and advocate for further reforms. This was ostensibly to lay the groundwork to force Paul Kruger, President of the Zuid-Afrikaanse Republiek, to accede to their demands. And in the process, the British Imperialist programme would bag the goldfields of South Africa.

Although Kruger and his government appeared receptive to demands, the conditions for the Uitlanders continued to deteriorate. Policemen on the streets were recruited from the surrounding farms, given arms, and with hardly an English word in their vocabulary, patrolled the streets of the mining town, applying the law with a heavy hand.

Cape Town

Cecil Rhodes, the Prime Minister of the Cape Colony, rose from behind his massive dark stinkwood desk, beautifully carved with ball and claw legs. A large painting of Queen Victoria hung behind him. Dr Jameson and John Hays Hammond entered his office, exhausted after the return trek from the goldfields. It was already well past midnight; everything was silent and deserted as the trio of men shook hands.

"Mr Hammond," Rhodes directed him to be seated. He acted on cue. Jameson, too, flopped down in a comfortable leather armchair. "I take it you aren't in Southern Africa for your health."

"No, Mr Rhodes," Hammond replied. "With due appreciation of the climate of this wonderful country, I do prefer that of California."

Rhodes nodded his understanding. "Now tell me—you've seen my properties on the Rand. What do you think of them?"

"Not very much, to be truthful, Mr Rhodes," Hammond drawled. "But, with your backing, I'm sure I could improve your investments without any difficulty."

"Are you absolutely sure?" asked Rhodes quizzically. Before Hammond could reply, he nodded, then said. "Johannesburg will die without the mines. How long do you think they'll last?"

Hammond paused for only a moment before replying. "Geologically, Mr Rhodes, there's no reason that the Rand shouldn't last at least fifty years and more. I foresee mines operating at depths of up to 5,000 feet vertically."

"My God, as deep as that!" exclaimed Jameson in surprise as he sat bolt upright in his chair.

"Sure, Doc." Hammond smiled. "I'll stake my reputation on it. And I'm not the only one who's convinced. There's your friend, Alfred Beit. He agrees with me. All we need is good government in the Transvaal and the land could be a treasure house for the entire world."

"Aha, a stable government," Rhodes interjected. "Just how do you think we're going to achieve that?"

A knowing smile flittered across Hammond's face. "Let's hope old Kruger will see some sense. Otherwise, you'll have to have it knocked into him. By God, it's two o'clock," Hammond exclaimed, glancing at his watch. "I'm off to get some sleep. Goodnight, Mr Rhodes, and to you, Dr Jameson."

Jameson rose and followed in Hammond's footsteps, yawning.

"No, don't go yet, Doc." Rhodes raised his voice as he glanced up. Slowly closing the open door, Jameson swung round, then sank back into the still-warm chair.

Jameson had been stationed in Kimberley as a doctor, and Kruger and the Matabele chief Lobengula had been his patients there and during that time, he met Rhodes.

Jameson left his medical practice and got involved in Rhodes's expansionist plans in then Rhodesia, becoming the chief magistrate and administrator in Mashonaland between 1891 and 1896. They had been friends for twenty years, but Rhodes was to prove to be a friend only when it suited him. Now it was time for Rhodes to discuss his plans for Jameson to invade the republic from the west.

"What do they think of me there?" Rhodes paced, and then gazed out at the night sky.

"They hate you," Jameson was candid.

"I suppose they are afraid," Rhodes muttered, considering his friend's reply. "Well, they have need to be. They had the best of the last business." He continued to pace, using Jameson as a sounding board. "Kruger is a strong personality, an overbearing man heading a dominant people. That's the trouble. Both the Dutch and the English are powerful nations, neither wanting to accommodate the other or live side-by-side. And Kruger is the man who fuels the Dutch determination." He thumped his clenched fist on a table to emphasise the point. "He is clever and astute. This time, he has beaten us all handsomely."

Now, he gripped the window still gazing into the darkness at the star-studded night. "I would control all the planets out there if I could." He reflected morosely as he gazed up into endless space. I often think of that."

"How long do you give him?" Jameson's question cut into Rhodes' thoughts.

"Who, Kruger?" Rhodes questioned.

"Who else?" replied Jameson.

"Three years," answered Rhodes without hesitation.

"Kruger has won the first rubber. When do you think the counter play will begin?"

The question caught Jameson off guard. He considered it for a few moments. "In three years?" he suggested. Still puzzled as to the whole point.

Rhodes smiled and shook his head. "No, you're wrong. Kruger won't fight for at least ten years. He is no fool."

He swung around to stare at Jameson. "So, they hate me in the Transvaal, even though they don't know me." He sighed and turned back to the window.

Jameson smiled at his friend's idealism. "Why don't you take up a stand on political grounds and show the Transvaal government that it's no longer possible to endure this intolerable state of affairs?" The idea seemed to excite him. He added, "Give me a few hundred Corporation men, and I'll make you a present of Johannesburg! We have 20,000 diggers on our side. The Boers would pack up and leave tonight!"

Rhodes stopped his pacing and considered the idea. Of course, the matter had crossed his mind, but it needed to be spelt out. It certainly wasn't that simple, though.

"Those Boers are not Matabele, Jim." He shook his head. "The only justification for revolution is success. Anyway, the Uitlanders have no arms. All the same, if the Johannesburg population–" He broke off and reconsidered. "–if the Uitlanders were to rise in revolt against the government, that might be the moment." He made a decision. "It looks very much, Jim as if you'd better call on some of my friends in Johannesburg."

Kate was busily arranging wild arum lilies in a vase. She glanced up, alarmed, as the door burst open. Francois stormed in angrily.

"What's it, Francois?" She asked anxiously. "Something went wrong?"

"Listen, Kate. If I tell you to leave with Josh, even if it's at an hour's notice, will you do it?"

Puzzled by Francois' serious manner, she replaced the flowers on the table and moved across the room towards him. "If you really want me to, but what's this all about?"

"There's the devil to pay in Pretoria," he fumed, thumping his fist violently on the armchair. "It was a shocking insult to the President. The Boers are hopping mad, and I don't blame them." His face was red with anger. "They're parading on horseback around the town in armed groups with guns loaded, looking as if they'd willingly shoot down every man, woman, and child. I believe it wouldn't take much to make Chamberlain intervene."

"Well, who wouldn't? We've every right," replied Kate indignantly. "If the Colonial Secretary can't soothe matters, then who can?"

Francois slumped into a chair. "It's not as simple as that. You must realise that intervention on the British part could mean war between Britain and the Transvaal. Then where would we and Johannesburg be?"

His question stung her into silence, but only for a moment. "Surely it wouldn't come to full-scale war. They wouldn't dare?"

"I wouldn't bet on that." He looked grim. "The Boers defied the British once before, at Majuba."

"Majuba," Kate flared. "That's all those Boers think about. If there'd been a Johannesburg then and 20,000 Uitlanders, it would have been a different story."

"Well, there are fewer than 1,000 rifles in the whole town." Francois chewed on his lower lip. "Probably no more than 500, which may all be necessary to defend ourselves against a Boer attack."

Kate edged over and sat on his knee as he reached out, cuddling her closer, allaying her fears. "Well, there's nothing much you can do about it right now, except buy another rifle and some more bullets. As we've only got one, don't you think we ought to be better prepared?" she asked, running her fingers through his hair.

"You're right." He smiled at her. "I'll get you a rifle during the week."

Her touch sent a feeling of weakness right through him. He found himself trembling with desire.

Kate stood up and began clearing the table. Francois watched her fluid movements. The voluptuousness of her breasts protruding from her dress was shadowed by the flickering candlelight. Her firm skin had taken on a rosy glow, but her slow and deliberate actions highlighted her conservatism towards Francois. Half sitting, half lying Francois watched as she removed the dishes. His eyes followed her about the room. She was certainly aware of him. They both knew it.

His eyes were wide and alive, as he rose and swept the tablecloth from the table. A flush came to her face as though she read his thoughts. Though unspoken, it was high time that they knew each other more intimately.

Slowly he moved towards her, gently drawing her back down onto the table. She shivered with a tingle of excitement to the gentleness of his touch. His hands stroked her thigh, and he began to kiss her.

The softness of her breasts against his chest excited him even more. His kisses covered her throat and moved down her stomach.

Kate did not remove his hand as they travelled down her back, playing with her spine, to finally cup her buttocks. She could feel him hardening against her, pressing closer.

It was not the lump in her throat that worried her as she struggled to catch her breath, while he started removing her undergarments, covering her mounds of smooth flesh with his tongue.

Kate felt right about this moment she had desired for so long. Her legs trembled as she was overwhelmed by the intensity of her passion, calling out, as he held her, the heat seeping through their bodies.

She tried to withdraw from him and turn away, embarrassed. She had never wanted anybody so much before. Her breasts heaved as her breath came in gasps. Before Kate could protest, Francois lifted her up, his hand sliding under her dress, between her legs, up along her smooth thighs, not stopping, not pausing. She knew where they were going. Part of her wanted them to stop. She cried out as he buried his face in her breasts, kissing her hungrily. She couldn't stop.

His hands felt under her remaining clothing, rubbing her dark patch, now into her round smooth slit as it swelled to meet him suddenly juiced with desire. She reached out, releasing his pants, and grabbed his bulging penis, holding it, caressing it, unable to let go.

The power of passion was plain. She responded with a fierce desire, wanting more and more of his embrace. Their kisses became deeper and lasted longer. She sighed as his fingers trailed over her lithe taut flesh. Somehow, she had always known that she would thrill to his touch.

The sight of her sensual, nubile body with its promise of ecstasy sent his pulse racing as the rest of her clothes fell in a heap. At the same time, he threw off his shirt and pulled off his trousers.

She gulped, her breath catching in her throat as his tongue travelled down to her clitoris, her hard button suddenly swelled, causing her to involuntarily buck as she yearned for it to move deeper while his hands caressed her bouncing, pouting breasts.

He grasped her waist, raising her towards him as his tongue slid back on to her mound, feeling her moistness as it probed deeper, dew-soft into her folds, her hands caressing and stroking his hair pushing his head deeper into her warm, furry pussy. Francois enjoyed her groans of pleasure, her nails bit into his forearms, his fingers clasped her nipples and caressed her breasts, an assurance of his own arousal.

His tongue slipped away from her as he moved upward, his penis sliding then thrusting inside her, throbbing, pulsating with the rhythm of their strokes, Kate could feel him growing. Her uncontrolled panting increased in volume as he searched the moist depths of her body, each movement heightening the intensity of their searing heat.

Glazed eyes gazed at each other in a sea of sweat and saliva, he bucking and she arching; now urgent, uncontrolled with the frenzy of their lust as if there was no end to it. A searing, burning sensation rose up, suddenly sweeping over both of them as they became one movement, time and space, their passion for each other spent.

Cigar smoke aromas drifted out from beneath Hammond's closed office door. In the middle of his desk on a square of blotting paper, stood a decanter of port. In front of each man was a crystal glass which they refilled periodically in conventional clockwise circuits. A map lay half unfolded and carelessly strewn upon the table as Phillips, Farrar and Hammond listened to Jameson. They drew on their cigars regularly and exhaled, sending smoke spiralling upward.

"There's no need to worry about a starting point," Jameson continued, watching them intently and trying to gauge their reactions. "Cecil Rhodes has fixed all that up. We've made a deal with both the black leaders, Montisoa and Ikaning, and we've got Pitsani in Bechuanaland."

The men peered intently at the map as Jameson unrolled it, using an inkwell to hold down the corner. He then drew a dark ring around the name of a small town. "That's where our forces will be stationed," he continued, half-smiling. "Well, it's all fairly straightforward. What's the arrangement from this end?" He gazed at their blank faces. Smoke hung thickly over the room.

George Farrar looked at the others, then rose. "While Hammond's outfit is raiding the arsenal, another bunch will head for West Church Street and Kruger's house."

"You not thinking of killing him?" Jameson blurted out, breaking off in mid-sentence and staring anxiously at Farrar.

"Course not, Doc," Farrar replied. "We're only going to kidnap him and bring him back to Jo'burg with us."

"We thought it would assist us in gaining our demands in any subsequent negotiations with the Boer government," Phillips interrupted. "Meanwhile, an old friend of ours, Francois du Plessis, has agreed to take a final petition to the Volksraad on our behalf."

Jameson smiled, stood up and raised his glass. Gentlemen, I congratulate you. You have audacity, simplicity and courage, the three essentials to success in war."

"Arms and ammunition are vital too," Hammond added dryly, holding his drink stationary in mid-air.

"We rely on Rhodes for those." Jameson took another sip.

Phillips held up his hand to still the excited chatter around the table. "Just a minute now." He exhaled cigar smoke. "Before we all go rushing off to Pretoria with six-shooters blazing, it seems to me there's a good chance of our getting away with a surprise raid on the arsenal. Even kidnapping Kruger, but after that, what? We'll have 20,000 well-armed and furious Boers encircling Johannesburg within two days."

Jameson answered quickly. "That's where Rhodes and I come in." He smiled, looking around at their blank faces.

"As soon as the signal for the revolt is given here, you must send a telegram to Rhodes and the High Commissioner in Cape Town. That'll be the only justification for the British government, and he'll be supported by Rhodes on behalf of the Cape. You also inform me at the same time, and I'll set off from Pitsani. It's what's known as protecting British lives and property." He finished his drink.

They'd go along with me, he thought. "I think that's all for the time being, gentlemen. I'll keep you informed of all developments. I don't have to impress on you the need for absolute secrecy. If Kruger suspects why that force is gathering at Pitsani, our whole plan will be ruined. I bid you a good day, gentlemen. Good luck!"

He gathered up the map on his way out, wishing to let them discuss what he had said. *They'll convince themselves*, he thought, closing the door behind him.

Phillips, now agitated, turned and stared at his subdued colleagues. "We've got to find out exactly where Cecil Rhodes stands on this. We can't afford any sort of misunderstanding!"

"I agree." Hammond nodded. "What's more, we've got to make sure that his objectives are the same as ours."

Pretoria Parliament

A dull murmur could be heard in the Volksraad as members waited with annoyance for additional demands from the gold diggers. These Uitlanders had invaded their quiet republic in their greedy pursuit of gold.

Here, in the bastion of Pretoria, their capital, these fortune hunters would never be permitted. Now the Raad was forced to listen to their continual griping and whining.

Francois rose to address the gathering of the Raad with their signed petition clasped in his right hand. "There is not a single man in this Raad who will use his powers more towards maintaining the independence of our land than myself," he began, "But I am convinced that it is the duty of this assembly to propose a modification of last year's law to deny the right to vote to the Uitlanders."

A ripple of dissent could be heard. Francois saw most of them shake their heads in disagreement. Motioned by the Chairman to continue, he grimaced and changed his strategy. He raised the petition aloft, which only served to increase the volume of disagreement.

"Who are the people who now demand a reasonable extension of the franchise?" His voice rose. "They include burghers from the Free State whose fathers, with yours, founded this country. They know no other fatherland, but the law still regards them as strangers!"

He felt their angry silence as he drew in a deep breath. "They have settled in this land for good. They have built Johannesburg. They own half the soil and pay nearly all the taxes. No wonder they have all banded together in one camp of hostility! The present law first compels them to wait fourteen years, and then pledges them nothing except a Volksraad decision in 1909!" He glared back at them. "Which one of you can say that this Volksraad will even be here then?"

A bedlam of dissent surfaced as Raad members leapt to their feet, fists clenched, hurling abuse threateningly at Francois as if he insulted their people by suggesting such an absurdity. He seethed as he watched them, sensing their antagonism and dislike for these same Uitlanders who had more than once insulted their President.

The sound of the Chairman hammering his gavel and shouting for order, surfaced above the chaos. Slowly the shouting subsided as Francois nodded his thanks. He continued sombrely. "I appeal to you as loyal burghers to open the door, if only a little, to these people. Not only for their sakes but also for ours. They will welcome the least generosity open-handed; I can assure you of that." As he sat down, a stony silence prevailed.

Everyone looked at Kruger, awaiting his reaction. Slowly, the elderly statesman rose. His expression was dour. "Let me say, Mynheer du Plessis, that these people who signed this monstrous petition are unfaithful and not law-abiding."

Francois leapt angrily to his feet. "I deny that!"

"They are traitors!" growled Kruger.

"They definitely are not," Francois retorted, standing his ground.

"Order! Order!" barked the Chairman, banging angrily with his gavel.

Kruger gazed around the chamber for their tacit approval before he glared at Francois. "I say these people are disrespectful and disobedient to the law because they are not citizens or even naturalised. Now, can anybody contradict that? No, you cannot. The law says you must be a burgher of the republic before you can petition this Raad, and these people are not burghers!"

In triumph, he beamed at the other Raad members, leaving Francois shaking his head in disagreement.

"I am against any extension except to those who go on commando. They show love for the country by making sacrifices for it," Kruger ranted. "The Raad might just as well give away the independence of this country as give all these newcomers the franchise!"

"How many times has the Raad heard that if the franchise isn't extended, there will be trouble?" General Piet Otto leapt to his feet angrily. As he interjected, his eyes blazed. "I am tired of all these threats. I say, if you want a fight, then come on!"

Several Raad members jumped to their feet, uttering their approval, denouncing the Uitlanders as pandemonium swept the Raad. The Chairman tried to restore some semblance of order as Otto continued in a booming voice.

No one heard the gavel. It was drowned out by his words of hatred. "The sooner, the better, Mynheer Chairman, I am prepared to fight them. I know every burgher of the Zuid-Afrikaanse Republiek is with me!" The Raad burst into hearty shouts of approval.

"Order, will you be quiet!" The Chairman shouted. "You have no right to say such a thing. We are not considering the questions of power, but the peaceful extension of the franchise. You must keep to the point, otherwise, I cannot allow you to continue."

"Very well, I'll step down," Otto growled as he retook his seat. "But I call on the whole country to witness that you silenced me and wouldn't allow me to speak my mind."

Now Kruger rose to his feet. "We have talked this question out. There is nothing more to be said. My counsel to the Raad is that you do not consent to Mynheer du Plessis' proposal. I don't want it put to the country. This business is reported every year until I am tired of it." He cleared his throat. "The will of the burghers is well known. The way open for Uitlanders to become burghers is clear. Let Mynheer du Plessis go back to Johannesburg and tell the people that if they are obedient to the law and become naturalised, they will not regret it."

Turning his back on the Raad, Francois stalked out of the Assembly. His footsteps echoed on the marble floor as the heavy wooden door closed noisily behind him.

CHAPTER 11

Wildflowers grew in pink, yellow and red profusion and thin grasses formed a delicate carpet. The shadows of the late November afternoon grew longer.

Alone on the grass koppie, Kate marvelled at the smooth, white arum lily petals and stroked them gently. Then breaking one off at the stem, she placed it among the sunflowers in her basket. The warm berg wind swirled around her ankles, causing her skirt to billow forth like a half-filled sail. She gazed up the hillside and noticed an egret perched high up in a crevice of the cliff face. Momentarily lost in thought, she literally spun around as she felt a hand on her shoulder. Her eyes widened in fright.

"Mel!" she exclaimed, her heart beating wildly. This man was Francois' enemy, he killed Pisani, she wanted nothing to do with him. "What are you doing here?"

"Come with me," he leered. "I'll show you my little cave, it's a beauty." He jerked his head up towards the hillside.

Kate extricated her hand from his grip and edged a pace backwards, her basket swaying against her side. "No, thanks. I'm busy picking flowers." Now her fear of him grew.

"Well, good on ya," replied Savage as he stepped closer. "But come, I'll show you where I stay."

Kate flinched from the smell of stale liquor on his breath. His dirty hand made for her mouth. "You hear me? I won't hurt you!"

Kate backed away. "I don't want to see your cave, so go away and leave me alone." She turned her back on him and walked off.

A peculiar expression crossed Savage's face. He grabbed her arm and pulled her towards him. Kate screamed, dropped her basket and struck out wildly with clenched fists. Scratching, she jerked her knee into his stomach. He lurched forward. His anger and his pain fanned the flames of his desire. Francois had routed him every time. Raping his woman would be the sweetest and most pleasurable form of revenge both for himself and Renzi's death.

Kate fought like a hellcat as he grabbed her again, but he was far too strong for her. He crushed himself against her body. She struggled, kicking and scratching, but his grip did not slacken. Pinning her down with his legs, Savage aimed a blow at her jaw. Her legs gave way from the single punch. Her head reeled in pain and confusion. Then she passed out. Savage took advantage of her weakness. Picking her up in his arms, he slung her over his shoulder, carrying her like a sack of potatoes. He wended his way high up the slope, pausing only once to catch his breath.

Kate became aware of a throbbing pain as she opened her eyes. The ground moved around her, and the blood rushed to her head as she gazed down at his scuffed leather boots. His huge hand grasped and tightened around her throat as she started to scream and kick again,

They reached a rock overhang halfway up the mountainside. Savage entered the cave through a narrow crevice. Then he unslung Kate and pushed her further inside into the darkness. A thin shaft of sunlight filtered through the cave opening. Still dazed and her heart thudding heavily, Kate took some moments to adjust to the blackness around her.

With a shock, she made out a charred heap of bones and at the far end some dirty blankets.

Savaged grabbed her. She tried to move, to run, but she was cornered and trapped. He pushed his foul-smelling mouth hard against hers while pawing at her dress. He ripped her bodice open with one mighty tug. Kate tried to tear herself free, but he yanked the dress down over her bare, trembling legs.

Kate writhed and screamed wildly, as Savage forced her down onto the blankets. His tongue rammed into her mouth, and his hands crushed her breasts. She screamed at the pain. He tugged at her panties, ripping them, then unbuckled his belt while his knees pinioned her down to the granite floor.

Savage pulled his fly open; he was going to get even. He was going to fuck her. He ground his teeth in victory as he thrust himself into her, grinding against her unwilling body. A rivet of pain coursed through her. Tears of helplessness welled in her eyes. She breathed in gulps as involuntarily her body movements took over. Her head lolled from side to side; she was trying to deny the awful experience she was suffering.

This sex act was so unlike the warmth she had felt with Francois. She now knew what it was to be violated and taken unwillingly. If only she could inflict some injury on him so he would stop! But she couldn't even move with the force of his weight on her.

Then suddenly, his grunting peaked; his release came. He rolled off her with a satisfied smile and pulled up his trousers. He walked towards the mouth of the cave and triumphantly looked back at her. Kate tried to cover her body with her tattered clothes, happy to regain some semblance of dignity. She shuddered as he chuckled. "I'm going out to get us a bottle of brandy, to loosen you up. Next time, you'll enjoy it far more."

Kate wanted to scream that nothing, even all the liquor in the world, would ever make her want him. Then she heard an even more ominous sound than his disgusting promises. Savage dragged a heavy rock and placed it against the mouth of the cave. "You can't get out, so don't even try."

Once the rock was in place, he started down the hillside.

Kate was enveloped in a shroud of darkness thicker and blacker than she had ever seen before. Its texture and weight crushed her from all sides. The silence around her was total. She sat enmeshed in a web of fear, brooding sombrely, drained of all light and song. The world of birds, trees, and laughter were as remote as a star as, helpless, she waited for his return.

Joseph looked around, surprised as he heard his name called above the noise of the bellowing cattle as he drove the herd along the dusty track. Behind him, the sun sank slowly and touched the treetops.

"Francois," Joseph smiled when he saw who had hailed him.

"Where's Kate?" Francois asked. He was still smarting from Kruger's rebuff.

Joseph sensed his friend's frustration and nodded his understanding as he rested his weight upon his staff. "She was picking flowers on the koppie. Isn't she back?" he inquired puzzled.

"No." Francois felt uneasy. "At least, I can't find her."

Joseph shook his head. "Something's wrong. We must go see!"

Both men made for their horses and rode through the cattle. It took only a few minutes of hard riding for them to reach the koppie. Their gaze swept across the green slopes, up over the rocky outcrops, as they shouted her name repeatedly.

Without warning, Joseph suddenly galloped off up the hillside.

"Where are you off to?" Francois shouted, urging his horse to follow.

Joseph remained silent, unsure of what he had seen, then pulled on the reins and came to an abrupt halt. He dismounted and examined Kate's empty basket and the trampled flowers, a knowing expression on his face.

Francois sucked in his breath. There had been some kind of struggle, so Kate must be in danger. But where was she now?

Joseph shielded his eyes from the setting sun as he squinted at the rock face. Suddenly he knew the answer. He pointed as he loped off up the slope. "Up there!"

"What is there?" Francois followed him with a wedge of fear lodged in his heart.

"The cave where my mother and I fled when the Bathlofiwa raided and killed my people many, many years ago."

Francois saw a heavy set of muddy footprints in the grass. Those surely didn't belong to Kate. Had a man carried her away and then accosted her? Francois became wild with anger. *Who had hurt his woman? Whoever it was would pay dearly.*

As they neared the cave, they noticed that a boulder now barred the entrance. Both men grabbed at the boulder and heaved with all their might. Slowly the barrier rolled away, and the mouth of the cave was open.

A woman's desperate cries reached them.

"Mama!" Joseph took a pace backwards, alarmed by the vision of his dead mother's ghost flittering through the cave.

"It's Kate!" Francois pushed him out of the way.

At the sight of Francois, Kate rushed into his arms, sobbing violently and trying to hide her naked body with her torn clothes.

"Are you hurt?" He held her gently and felt her body shake all over.

She shook her head as tears welled. "Only a little."

Thank God, she was alive.

"Who did this to you?" he demanded, livid beyond all reason.

"Savage," she stuttered. "I tried to stop him but he ..."

"I know what he did." Francois' voice was as cold as ice. The thought of his avowed enemy touching and forcing his filth into Kate's beautiful body made his blood boil with rage. "Where is the bastard now?"

"He said he was going to get liquor." She gulped and shivered. "He was so disgusting. Just the thought of him touching me ..."

"We'll take her back to the hotel," Francois directed Joseph. He took off his coat and held it out to her. "Then we'll look for Savage! I'll lead the posse."

Francois lifted Kate into his arms and carried her out into the fresh air. By God, he swore, this time Savage would pay with his life.

The posse rode into the bushveld, grim determination on their faces and revenge in their hearts. An eye for an eye, the good book told them. It was now time to even the score.

Joseph cast a concerned glanced at Francois. He galloped ahead of Rogaly, Hammond, Farrar and Phillips with a murderous glint frozen over his features.

They rode rhythmically, eating up the veld; the horses' hooves pounding the dry, cracked ground. No one spoke. The jingle of stirrups cut through the silence as they made their way up the hill towards the cave.

The heavy pummelling of the beasts on the earth reverberated through the cave. Savage emerged in a drunken stupor from the opening. His bloated face was flushed and dirty, his eyes bloodshot. He saw the dust cloud thrown up by the horses' hooves and knew the men astride those beasts were out to get him. He lurched towards the mountainside as he tried to climb to the top, out of reach. In his panic, he scrambled and scratched his way up the rocky outcrop, dislodging pebbles. His fear of their retribution gave him renewed strength as he clawed at the jutting ledge.

In this land, he knew that justice and revenge were swift and fatal. Savage gazed around wildly. His chest heaved, and his head swam with fear. The emotion contorted his ugly features as he watched the posse rein in at the base of the koppie.

He clawed at the rock ledge, desperate to get away. But the face of the hillside was too smooth and too sheer. His fingers lost their traction. Now he slid down in a shower of pebbles and was trapped, alone on the ledge.

He gazed spellbound as the group of men dismounted, all brandishing hunting rifles. He was their prey.

"Give yourself up! We promise you justice and a fair trial in court," Phillips shouted, remaining in the saddle with his rifle cradled in his arms.

Savage made no reply. He shook with fear. Trapped like an animal, he slunk back against the rock face.

Rogaly coughed, drawing Lionel's attention. "It's impossible to get up there and throw a rope."

"Well, then." Farrar glanced from man to man. "We'll have to do something before darkness falls."

"Leave it to me." The men fell silent as Francois strode forward, rifle in hand, a determined glint in his eye. The others knew better than to interfere. "Savage!" Francois called out. "This is du Plessis. Get off that damn ledge, or I'll shoot you down." He paused. "You know I'll do what I say."

There was no movement from Savage.

"You have ten seconds to move." He started counting. Savage stayed where he was.

Francois mechanically slid the cartridge into the breech. There was no rush as he took aim while he counted. Time seemed to stand still as the others held their breath, waiting. "Nine, ten. That's it, Savage!" Francois bellowed. "Time's up." His right index finger squeezed the trigger.

The bullet whined its way as if in slow motion to its target; Savage instinctively moved backwards. His head jerked upward as the bullet whistled past him and smashed into the rock, shattering it into a shower of free-flying pebbles.

He took another step forward, trying to shield himself from the fall-out. For a single moment, he swayed as he glanced downward. Then he lurched forward in a panic. His foot slipped. Losing his balance, he grabbed desperately at the ledge. His hand seemed to grip the ridge as he dangled in space, then Savage plunged. His scream of fear slashed through the silence as he hurtled towards the base of the cliff.

He plummeted headlong onto the rocky outcrop with a thud. The body bounced as it hit the unyielding stone. Savage twitched as he landed as if trying to toss off the pain. Then all movement ceased as life was crushed and broken.

For a few moments there was a stunned silence among the men. Wheeling his horse around and without looking back, Francois rode out. Silently the others followed suit. Rogaly was the first to speak. "He was warned. He wouldn't listen."

"We know," Phillips butted in. "Nobody will miss him."

"Especially me," Francois retorted. A burial was too good for Savage. He would leave the bastard to the vultures.

The sky burnt a fiery sienna orange in the glowing sunset while a cold easterly wind whipped up the riders' coattails as their horses' hooves drummed out their own tune.

Some days later, Farrar, Phillips, Hammond and Francois poured over the map Jameson had spread out on Hammond's desk.

"Well, Lionel," Jameson looked at Phillips. "If you can arrange supplies of food and water for the horses and men at those three points, you can leave the rest to me. Will you be able to sort it out?"

Phillips nodded. "It's all in hand, Doc. You remember Victor Woolf? Well, he's arranged to buy a couple of hundred horses in case you need any remounts. He's let it be known that he's starting a coach service between Mafeking and Johannesburg." Phillips stubbed at a point on the map with his finger. "That's where they'll be waiting, about halfway between the towns. At a farm that belongs to a man named Malan who's agreed to look after them." A grin spread over his face. "Incidentally, Malan's a member of the Volksraad."

"Well, I'm blowed," Jameson chuckled. "Tell Woolf I think he's done a sterling job. Now, we've got to decide on a date." He looked around at the others, waiting for suggestions.

Hammond blew a smoke ring. "We know we can be sure of you and Rhodes. But what about the Home Secretary Chamberlain, and the Home Government?"

Jameson shifted uncomfortably; his chair creaked as he leant forward, a convincing fixed smile now playing on his face. "I think I can set your mind at rest on that score. As you know, I'm Sir Hercules Robinson's physician, and he's the Cape Governor. You can take it that he knows every detail of the arrangement.

"And Chamberlain?" Francois queried.

"His position is not an easy one, as you can imagine. He knows what's going on, of course, and approves. Still, he won't be able to give his official support until your uprising has been successful and he thinks that the time is ripe for the government to intervene. All right, du Plessis?"

A ripple of relieved laughter surfaced and broke the tension. "Good, now we've got to settle on a date. I'll need another fortnight to complete my arrangements." He searched the calendar. "Say, between Christmas and New Year? How about December 28th?"

Phillips glanced at the others, who nodded. "That date will do provisionally. What we'd better do is call a public meeting for the 28th, at which time we'll announce our 'Manifesto'. That'll be the ultimatum to Kruger and the signal for you to start. But there's one thing we feel we must make quite clear," he added, on a more serious note. "Under no circumstances are you to cross the border until you get the word from us. That must be clearly understood."

Jameson hesitated, drawing on his cigar. He absorbed the tone of the warning. "We must aim for a simultaneous movement here in Jo'burg and at my end. The signal will be given by you, of course. In the meantime, I'll carry on, on the assumption that December 28th is the day. For heaven's sake, remember that if the Transvaal government gets word of this and starts moving troops to the border, I might have to jump the gun," He paused to let the impetus of his words sink in. "I'll need a letter of sorts from you people. I already mentioned this to Lionel. Have you told them?"

Phillips nodded. "I've discussed it with Farrar, and we've drafted a letter addressed to you." He handed the white square to Jameson. "It is necessary that they should know that they're coming at the invitation of the people of Johannesburg to rescue their countrymen from a situation of grave danger. I'm sure you understand."

Jameson skimmed through the contents, stroking his ginger moustache. Then he smiled. "That'll do me very well. It explains the situation in a nutshell, if I may say so, Lionel. All it needs now are your signatures."

"What about the date?" Francois frowned.

"Well, I've omitted that," Phillips explained. "It is understood among us that this letter will be used for no other purpose than already stated. And it's not to be used without our instruction. At that time, we can also inform Dr Jameson of the date to be put on the letter."

"Well then, gentlemen, please sign. Will you start, Farrar?" Jameson suggested.

Ignoring Jameson, Francois interjected. "Giving Jameson an undated letter of foolish rhetoric can lead to dangerous complications. I'm sorry gentlemen, I cannot sign such a document." He sat back in his chair, lips drawn and taut, as he watched and waited.

Both Phillips and Farrar leant forward and scribbled their signatures. Hammond hesitated, looked across at the two men, then at Francois, as if weighing the consequences. Then he too signed. Francois remained motionless with his arms folded defiantly.

Jameson pocketed the letter, finished his drink and rose. "Thank you, gentlemen. You need have no worries for the future. You play your part, and I'll play mine."

"Not before we tell you to!" Hammond warned. "This is not an invasion. You come by invitation only."

Jameson laughed at the suggestion as he brushed aside the warning. "It's like coming to a party. I agree and accept. Good-bye, gentlemen. When we meet again, it will be to hoist the Union Jack over the Government Building in Pretoria!" He strode from Hammond's office.

Francois growled. "What did he mean by that, hoisting the Union Jack? If this is an uprising on behalf of the British Empire, you can count me out!"

CHAPTER 12

Cape Town

Jameson reached the elegant sandstone Rhodes building on St George's Street, opposite the cathedral. The black iron gables stood out in front of each window. Above him, Table Mountain was covered with a tablecloth of cloud sweeping down its slopes. This was a sign of the dreaded south-easter and the vicious wind whipped at his trouser legs. It was a relief to get inside.

Rhodes was waiting for him. "Come inside." He peered quickly down the corridor. "We don't know who's watching us." He walked to the window and closed them. "Now what can you tell me?"

Jameson draped his coat over the back of the chair. His attention was caught by the mast of the schooner sailing in Table Bay, with its billowing sails battling against the wind.

"The Uitlanders are adamant that we must not make a move until this question of the flag is settled. And in the way they want it."

"And that, I take it," Rhodes surmised, "means no Union Jack or Corporation flag."

"That's correct."

"Damn!" Rhodes exclaimed in frustration. He pounded his fist into the desktop. Then he threw his hands up in disgust and paced the room. "What do these Uitlanders expect? They are only interested in making money. Tell me," he paused and stopped his agitated steps, "Is there no one in Johannesburg who will risk being shot at, and who will lead the revolt?"

Jameson reflected briefly, and then shook his head. "There's no one suitable if their present mood continues."

"Well, if they won't, that's out." Rhodes began to pace again, then halted and smiled as he reached his decision. "You can tell the Uitlanders that I agree, but I want you to understand that when the proposed revolt takes place, it will be under the British flag."

Johannesburg, December 25th

Lionel Phillips contemplated his eggs and bacon without much appetite. He swatted the flies, which shared all his meals, more viciously. The morning paper was propped up against the marmalade jar. He had just started to pour himself a cup of coffee when the door to his cabin flew open. Francois was framed by the sunlight in the doorway.

"Where's the Baas?" Francois joked.

"Having breakfast," Phillips retorted cheerfully, his sour mood suddenly changing.

"Good, I'll have some coffee with him." He smiled, then drew up a stool and sat down.

"Merry Christmas, Francois," Phillips grinned, extending a hand.

"And the same to you, Lionel. Though I don't know what's merry about it." He seemed somewhat subdued as he grasped Phillips' outstretched hand.

Phillips surveyed his friend. "What's bothering you?" He poured a mug of piping hot coffee.

Francois nodded his thanks and took a sip. "I was talking to Hammond last night. He told me that he was sure Jameson was going to come in under the Union Jack. Look here, Lionel, I haven't been in on all your meetings, but if Jameson is coming to hoist the Union Jack, then I'll have no part of it. What we want is still a republic, but a reformed one." He took another sip. "Listen, Lionel, this is a Boer country. It's morally wrong to think of doing anything that would change the republic's status. I will not go one yard further in the business unless I have the assurance from you and the others that this is the basis for the uprising."

Phillips nodded and wiped his gold-rimmed spectacles clean. "I can give you that assurance as far as I'm concerned, and I think I can speak for the others. But whether that's going to have an effect on Jameson is a different matter. Rhodes is the only man who can stop him now, I'm afraid."

Francois grimaced. The whole affair reeked. "I suggest that we postpone it all until we're sure of what we're doing."

"All right, I'll put it to the others," Phillips drained his coffee mug, "that we send an ultimatum to Kruger. Meanwhile, how about Josh riding over to Jameson? We'll order him to wait on the border until he receives instructions from us."

"Okay." Francois rose. "But there's to be no Union Jack!"

Pretoria

President Paul Kruger drew on his pipe and placed his Bible on the table as he waited for General Piet Otto to approach him.

"Your Honour," Otto greeted him. "Is it true what I hear? That there may be rebellion in Johannesburg? There is much talk." He drew up a chair alongside Kruger.

"It's true, General." Kruger exhaled a puff of smoke.

"Well, Your Honour," Otto leaned forward, hat in hand. "I have many bullets lodged inside me from the War of Independence, but I can make for a few more if it's a question of fighting those *rooineks* again!"

Kruger looked at him solemnly. "I do not think you will need to do that, General. I too have heard all the stories from Johannesburg, but I don't have to believe them. You don't have to believe every lion story you hear, do you?" he added, raising his bushy eyebrows. "Just keep your guns clean and your horse in the stable."

"But, Oom Paul," Otto protested vigorously. "Why not fall on them at once?"

Kruger was not the sort of person to be easily pushed around. It was probably the first time in his life that he had been confronted in such a manner. He was an intelligent man who knew that he was facing an adversary that could indeed bring down his government. He knew that the British government would step in, grab the goldfields, and annex his small country without hesitation if there was a revolution.

Kruger leaned back and laughed heartily, then shook his head. "If you want to kill a tortoise, you must first wait until it puts its head out of the shell; only then can you cut it off. *Met geduld en moed, alles sal regt komen.*" (With courage and patience, all shall be overcome.)

He got up and walked out onto the wide wooden stoep. Suddenly his expression soured as he caught sight of Hammond striding down the street towards them. His fashionable pin-striped suit and smart white hat out of place, contrasting sharply with the dull, conservative clothes worn by the Boers. He sighed. "And now, the deputation from Johannesburg is coming." He motioned Otto to remain seated.

At first, Kruger ignored Hammond and remained on the stoep. Then he slowly turned and faced Hammond. "Now Oom Paul is among you." His voice was deep. "Ask or tell me what you want. Speak."

"Your Honour," Hammond began. "I come on behalf of the people of Johannesburg, as it were, with a rifle in one hand and an olive branch in the other. If the peace offering is accepted, we'll say: Take our guns, we trust you." He paused as he waited for a reply.

Kruger sighed wearily and removed his pipe from his mouth. "When Mynheer Barnato wants anything, he always comes to see me himself, and we talk it over. You others always send deputations to Pretoria." Kruger's eyes narrowed as he watched Hammond. He tried to manoeuvre him into his territory, slow down the negotiations and expose any weakness.

Barnato met with Paul Kruger, President of the Transvaal Republic for the first time in 1889. They met subsequently, and a friendship developed. He had presented Kruger with the pair of decorative stone lions which now graced the entrance to Kruger's Pretoria house on Church Street.

Hammond chose his words carefully. "It was difficult for the others to come, so they sent me."

Kruger puffed on his pipe; the smoke spiralled upward. "Let us discuss, then," he added noncommittally. Knowing his love for conversing and his simplistic art of twisting points of friction to his advantage, Hammond moved directly to the causes of the diggers' agitation.

"Equality of Dutch and English."

Kruger jabbed his pipe in Hammond's direction. "This is a Dutch Republic, founded, civilised and reclaimed by the Dutch. Dutch is the official language, but English is and can be spoken freely everywhere, in the council of law and other offices of administration."

"Removal of religious disabilities," Hammond continued.

"The law of this country allows every man to worship and think as he pleases." His mouth was set in a rigid line. "Only the holders of office and public officials must be Protestants." Satisfied with his reply, he waited for the next complaint.

"Independence for the Courts of Justice," Hammond continued.

"We all want that. I am thankful to say we have it," Kruger responded.

"Liberal and comprehensive education," Hammond read the fourth complaint.

Kruger measured his words before replying. "If people want English education for their children, let them pay for it. I will do my part, but it cannot be expected that a Dutch government will treat its own language as a foreign one."

Hammond kept tight control on his rising anger. Taking a deep breath, he added, "Lastly, equitable franchise law and fair representation."

Alerted, Kruger smiled and pointed the butt of his pipe in Hammond's direction. "This is the only real grievance you can complain of. But you don't want any franchise under a republic. It is merely an excuse to further Rhodes' schemes. It is in our interest to keep the peace, but if our independence has to go, it must be taken by force. Even if it was granted, how many Englishmen would give up their birthright and take an oath of allegiance to the republic?" He broke off and waited for a reply.

None was forthcoming.

"However, I will do my best when the Volksraad next meets, to reduce the minimum period required for the Second and maybe the First Chamber. I must tell you," his eyes narrowed, "that my efforts to get concessions for the Uitlanders have been spoiled by their foolish and threatening talk and actions."

Hammond stared back coldly, waiting for the President to pause before interrupting him. "The issue of war or peace is in your hands. I earnestly trust that as a prudent and practical statesman, you will decide in favour of peace."

"No!" Kruger erupted angrily. His complexion darkened and his angry features now matched his sombre clothing. "They want to wrench the rod of government out of my hands and hit me over the head with it. Rhodes and Chamberlain mean to fight me. I am preparing for battle."

Understanding that renewed hostilities with Britain were now a real possibility, Kruger had already begun to pursue armaments, ordering rifles and munitions from Germany which was in direct conflict with Britain's expansionist African policies

"With your permission, Mr President," Hammond responded coolly. "There's no danger at hand unless the government creates it. If Your Honour dealt with the people more liberally, you wouldn't find a more loyal community in the world than the inhabitants of Johannesburg."

"You Uitlanders were never intended to settle in the Transvaal." His tone was glacial. "Nor are you wanted here. Why don't you leave and let us breed our cattle and farm in peace?"

"And where did you get your land from?" Hammond was angered by Kruger's insinuations as he rose to his feet.

Furious at this disrespect, General Otto jumped to his feet and confronted Hammond. "I got it where you got your ugly face from, my father," growled Otto rudely.

"I beg your pardon. My father was a gentleman and a governor." Hammond snapped back, offended by the insult.

"And my father was a shepherd," Kruger responded in a mocking tone. He leaned forward triumphantly. Then he relaxed back into his chair and drew on his pipe. "Tell me, Mynheer Hammond, if a crisis should occur, on which side shall I find the Americans?"

"They would support liberty and good government." Hammond's reply was brief as he sensed that Kruger was about to gain the upper hand.

"You're all alike, tarred with the same brush. At heart you are no different to the British," Kruger grumbled. Then he coughed and spluttered, and pulled out a handkerchief. "I want no such war. But just suppose you are going down a road with nothing but a pocketknife and you meet a lion. Would you be so reckless as to attack it with such a weapon? Certainly not! But suppose that lion attacked you, you would be forced to defend yourself with it. Not so?" He raised his bushy eyebrows in an enquiry.

"All we want in this country is a transparent administration and an equitable share in the voice of its affairs," Hammond tried to interject.

"*Nee, nee, nee!*" Kruger leant forward. Now his dark eyebrows were drawn in towards the bridge of his nose. "Let me finish speaking, Mynheer. You don't want reforms! What you really desire is my country! While I live, I mean to prevent you from having it!" He inhaled deeply, then exhaled through his teeth as he tried once more to reason with Hammond. "Listen, if I give a man a ride in my coach, he is welcome. But what if he says, 'Hand over the reins.' I cannot do that, for I know not where he will drive me." He wagged a finger at Hammond. "You Uitlanders make it your business to keep Johannesburg in a constant state of ferment. Apparently, you are agitating for the franchise, but your real objective is a very different one, as we shall see."

Hammond shook his head to deny the charges. "No, you're wrong!"

His retort further angered Kruger. "All right, if you want your rights, why don't you fight for them?" He started to shout. "Go back and tell your people that I'll never change my policy. And now let the storm burst!"

CHAPTER 13

Kate kissed Francois tenderly. The springs of the brass bed squeaked. She smiled as they drew apart; a warm wave of contentment enveloped her as she stared into the growing darkness, then frowned as she nestled back against the pillows. "I listened to some Boers talking in the square. From how they behaved, it seems to me that resentment is running high against the English. Do you think there will be a war?"

Francois propped himself on one elbow and tried to allay her fears. Lovingly he stroked her forehead as he spoke. "It's not likely. All they want is reforms. They're only assembling Jameson's force as a show of strength; there's no question of their bringing them in."

"Where do you stand if war comes?" Her face was etched with worry. "You are a Boer, aren't you?"

"Well, yes, I am," he sighed, sinking slowly back onto the pillow. "My grandfather farmed in the Free State, but my father grew tired of life on the land. He went down to Durban, where he married my mother, who was English. I was born there. So, what does that make me?"

"It makes you an Afrikaner, a Boer." She nodded. "And that makes me a Boer too," she reflected. "Although what I now consider myself will hardly affect the issue."

Francois sighed. "I suppose that if it came to the push and both Rhodes and Jameson came in uninvited, I would fight for my own people. I would have to make an effort if I thought I should."

They gazed at each other. Neither needed war nor separation to tear them apart. They embraced, secure in their love for each other but perturbed about the potential chaos around them.

Pitsani, Bechuanaland

Dust bowls eddied round as gusts of warm, dry air blew in from the north. The 700 Corporation men mustered excitedly outside their tent town, with the small village of Pitsani visible in the distance. They busied themselves, oiling artillery, cleaning rifles and preparing for the invasion. Besides their rifles, they had plenty of Maxim machine guns and a number of light artillery pieces.

The basic plan was that Johannesburg would revolt and seize the Boer armoury in Pretoria. Jameson and his force would dash across the border to Johannesburg to "restore order", and with control of Johannesburg they would control the goldfields. They hoped that this would be a three-day dash to Johannesburg before the Boer commandos could mobilise and trigger an uprising by the Uitlanders.

The excitement of the recent Bulawayo campaign still lived with them. They were Rhodes' men and had taken over and named Rhodesia after him. Now they would do the same thing with the puny Transvaal Republic.

Overhead the sun burnt their fair skins as they lived up to their insulting "rooinek" name. *This drive had better be successful*, Rhodes contemplated as he reflected upon his long, hot and dusty journey up from the Cape. In front of him, the men scurried around, buttoning up their blue tunics as they scrambled for position. *Pity they couldn't have been wearing the red militia uniform of British soldiers*, he thought. *Still, they had experienced annexing Rhodesia for the Empire, and they were his Corporation men.*

He smiled as Jameson joined him. Watching the men, he suddenly recalled another ancient and classic confrontation as he muttered the verse.

And they stood there on the meadow
With their weapons and their war-gear
Wildly glaring at each other:
In their faces stern defiance
In their hearts the feud of ages
The Song of Hiawatha, Henry W. Longfellow

"Go stand the men easy, Doc," he directed, returning to reality.

Assembling the troops, Jameson, dressed in a fawn-coloured coat, a short, slight figure, with a pale face wearing a well-clipped moustache, nervous brown eyes, and a boyish grin. But his voice was a magnet.

He had them stand at ease as Rhodes walked over, taking up a central position. He faced them, hands in pockets as he addressed them. His voice carried on the breeze. "Well, men, you've had a long wait. Now it's over. Most of you will have seen the Reuters messenger from Johannesburg. What many of us feared would happen, has now occurred. Your countrymen are in great peril through insisting on rights and reforms which are the birthright of all Britons." He paused to let the essence of what he had said sink in before continuing. "We know now that women and children are fleeing from the danger which surrounds them as Boer forces begin their encroachment of the town. Perhaps even as I talk to you, the first shots are being fired, and British blood is flowing in the streets of Johannesburg. We can delay no longer."

Jameson pulled out the letter from his inside jacket pocket, opened it and waved it aloft. It was a kind of passport, an invitation from the committee of Uitlanders organised by Rhodes and Beit and the mine owners and other businesses who represented British interests in the town. The letter was undated, supposedly for the moment after the uprising in the town had begun.

It would cover them with both the Chartered Company and the Imperial government in case there were awkward questions. It was a gamble. If they lost, they would be sentenced to death. If they won, they would march into Johannesburg and Pretoria triumphantly, and the British government would annex the Transvaal, and probably banish Kruger.

"I have here a letter from the leaders of the Uitlanders." Holding it at arm's length, he began reading aloud. "Thousands of unarmed men, women and children of our race are at the mercy of well-armed Boers. It is under these circumstances that we feel obliged to call upon you to come to our aid."

Tucking the letter back into his pocket, he continued. "The critical moment for Johannesburg has arrived. I do not believe that the Boers are aware of our plans. I want to impress upon you that this is not an attack on the Boers or the Transvaal Republic. We are going to the relief of our countrymen in peril." He paused to gauge the men's reaction.

"Sir," one of the troopers called out. "Are we going to fight for the Queen?"

Rhodes fixed his gazed upon the soldier, then looked at all the others around him. "No, you are not actually going to fight for the Queen, but for the supremacy of the British flag in South Africa. There is no compulsion on anybody to come with us, but I am confident that all of you will respond to this call from your countrymen. I have asked Dr Jameson to reassemble the parade at sundown, mounted and in full marching order. I hope you have a pleasant ride."

"Three cheers for Cecil John Rhodes," Jameson shouted, moving forward, to a chorus of hearty cheers echoing across the veld.

Satisfied, Rhodes smiled his thanks and turned. Immediately, his attention was diverted towards the lone horseman, riding hard with dust flying in his wake.

Jameson stole a quick glance at Rhodes as they watched the rider approach. The men, too, peered inquisitively in their ranks.

Josh reared up, filthy with dust after his long ride from Johannesburg. Dismounting rapidly, he strode over to Jameson, a letter clutched in his hand.

Jameson looked at Rhodes, who remained unmoved at Josh's approach. He jerked his head in Rhodes' direction. "Take it to Mister Rhodes."

"No, Dr Jameson had better read it," Rhodes retaliated.

No sooner had Josh done an about-turn than Jameson retorted. "Mister Rhodes is in military command, let him read it."

Grinning Rhodes made his way over to Jameson. "Come on, Doc, you're in charge." Then he noticed young Josh, pale. "You look like a ghost. Are you all right, man?"

"I've ridden all night, sir, and covered eighty miles. I was stopped by the Boers at Malmani and held up for four hours."

"The devil you were!" Rhodes exclaimed, his eyes brightening. "You hear that, Doc? How many were there?"

"It was the magistrate Marais with four or five men," Josh answered with respect.

"Well, you had better get some breakfast," Rhodes advised, as he placed a fatherly arm on Josh's shoulder.

But Josh stood his ground. "I have orders to take back a reply to the message, sir."

Rhodes sighed, took the letter and scanned its contents. Then he glanced back at Jameson. "What should we tell them then, Doc? It's just what we expected."

"Better say the despatch has been received and that we'll attend to it."

Josh interrupted, intent on making a point. "I must take back a fuller reply, sir."

"Very well," Rhodes relented. "I'll dictate. Are you ready?"

Taking a notebook and pencil from his breast pocket, Josh nodded.

"Very well then, Rhodes began. "What is the date? December the 26th?" He cleared his throat. "Sirs, I am in receipt of your protest of the above date and have to inform you that we intend proceeding."

The bugle sounded. Jameson mounted a black stallion. He took off his felt hat, and there were three ringing cheers for the Queen. Then they trotted out of Pitsani, followed by the African servants and the mule carts. The moon had risen, flashing on the tin walls of the village and the brass-and-steel mountings of the eight Maxims and three field guns, before the column of eleven mule carts and thirty packhorses was engulfed in dust.

Johannesburg

A tense air of confusion and uncertainty was evident in the hallway and even in Hammond's office as both Hammond and Farrar hastily opened the telegrams, ripping the envelopes with carved wooden letter openers.

"It's from Rhodes," Hammond announced aloud. "Some of it is in code. Won't be a minute." He drew out the codebook from his desk drawer.

Farrar frowned as he handed over his telegram. "Mine's from Jameson. Will you decipher this one too?"

A worried expression clouded Hammond's gaze as he deciphered the telegram, then, with a sigh of relief, slammed the codebook down on the table. "Well, it's all right at Cape Town, thank goodness. This is what the telegram says. 'I have received perfectly satisfactory assurances from Dr Jameson, but a misunderstanding undoubtedly exists elsewhere. In my opinion, continue preparations, but an entirely fresh departure will be necessary. Jameson has been advised accordingly.' That's from Rhodes, and I think you'll agree it means Rhodes has ordered Jameson to wait."

Farrar was relieved. "What about the doctor? What does he say?"

Puzzled, Hammond scratched his head. "I can't quite make it out. Seems a bit muddled to me." He frowned, scratching his head again before returning it and the codebook to Farrar. "Here, George, you may know what it means. You read it."

Puzzled, Farrar cross-checked it with the codebook. He jotted down its meaning, then re-examined it. "Blimey, I dunno. Most of it is gibberish. It must have got mixed up in the telegram office. But this is clear enough. I shall start without fail tomorrow night."

Hammond glanced up. "What time was it sent?"

Farrar scanned it again. "At 2:30 yesterday afternoon."

"Then it doesn't really matter, does it? The doctor must have sent that before he'd heard from Josh and Rhodes." Hammond responded.

"You're right." Farrar nodded a bit too quickly, still uneasy.

"Whatever Jameson had in mind yesterday afternoon he couldn't possibly start in defiance of our wishes and against the orders of Cecil Rhodes. But what a good thing we made sure. Phew, I feel like a drink." Hammond mopped his brow.

As they were gathering up their jackets, Francois burst angrily through the doorway. He too clutched a telegram in his hand and waved it in front of him. "Who the hell is Godolphin?" He demanded. "Have we got a man in Cape Town called that? Is it a code name?"

"Just a minute, Francois." Hammond was puzzled. "Just what is in this telegram?"

Francois confronted him. "You may well ask! Just listen to this. It's addressed to me from Cape Town and was despatched at 7:30 this morning. Remember that." Now he read the contents. "The veterinary surgeon says that the horses are now all right. Stop. He started with them last night. Will reach you on Wednesday. Stop. He says he can back himself for 700. Godolphin." Francois snorted. "What the hell do you make of that?"

"Are you quite sure of the time?" Hammond queried.

"See for yourself." Francois' reply was terse. "There's no mistaking, half-past seven this morning. We know who the veterinary surgeon is, but who the hell is Godolphin? The telegram must mean that Jameson left Pitsani with seven hundred men."

Unless it's a terrible joke." Hammond interjected as the tension increased in the room.

"I think Godolphin is the name of the school Jameson attended. It's all too preposterous," Farrar blustered. "Jameson can't be that mad!"

"I agree with you, George." Hammond stammered and shook his head in disbelief. He searched for an alternative explanation. "Rhodes would have stopped him, even if we couldn't." He glanced over at Farrar for his approval.

Furious Francois thumped the desk. "The bastards have tricked us. They are coming! They intend to run up the Union Jack!" His face contorted with anger. "I won't play a part in this."

"It's all up, boys. He's started in spite of everything." Phillips called out as he entered the room and threw the telegram on the desk. "Read this: The contractor has started the earthworks with 700 boys. Stop. Hopes to reach terminus on Wednesday. Jenkins."

Francois snatched up the message. "I see this one came from Mafeking, timed at noon. Who is Jenkins?"

"One of my men at Mafeking, absolutely reliable," Phillips replied, suddenly tired from tension. He sunk into the chair. He tried to resign himself to the gravity of the situation.

"Well, gentlemen!" Francois was barely able to control his temper. "That's that. Jameson and his troops have been riding for nearly twenty-four hours. You can't stop them, but can you prevent a war? That's your next problem."

Their feud was interrupted as Rogaly entered.

"What's Rogaly got hold of?" Francois demanded as Rogaly held out yet another telegram.

"Kruger's planning to withdraw the Zarps from Jo'burg. They'll have to, won't they, if anything starts. That would be sensible." Francois snorted at Rogaly's naive analysis.

They all heard the newspaper boy cry outside: *Extra! Extra! Jameson nears border! Conflict imminent! Extra!*

"The goddamn fool," Hammond hissed.

An air of despondency settled over the room. Jameson wasn't invited, yet he was coming.

Phillips regained his composure. He was once again alert. "We must form a committee of action. I propose to send a telegram to the High Commissioner and Cecil Rhodes, in his capacity as Prime Minister of the Colony, informing him of our position here."

"We must be very careful about this, Lionel," Hammond chimed in. "If any rumours get out that the High Commissioner is on his way to run up the Union Jack, you'll have to count me out. As well as every other American, German, and Frenchman in town. Now, if Robinson was invited here as a mediator to prevent bloodshed," a grin creased the edges of his mouth, "that would be different."

Phillips nodded. "Of course." He turned to Farrar. "George, get this telegram off to the High Commissioner of Cape Town with a copy to Rhodes . . . 'Owing to premature start Jameson with armed force into Transvaal. Stop. Johannesburg placed in a position of extreme peril which completely unprepared to meet. Stop. Urge High Commissioner proceed immediately to Johannesburg and Pretoria to negotiate peaceful settlement and prevent civil war. Stop'. Better sign that Lionel Phillips for Reform Committee so that he doesn't think I'm acting on my own. Put it in code, George."

He stared at Francois. "Will you take a message to the President?" He paused, trying to gauge his mood and appeal to his sense of fairness. "For what it's worth, we've all been tricked. We never intended a civil war." He let the words sink in. "As the Johannesburg representative in the Volksraad, you're the only person Kruger may listen to."

The plea hung in the air as Francois angrily scowled. "Just tell him we don't want a civil war. But we'll do it to get reforms that the government won't give us." He squared his shoulders. "We've always offered the olive branch and tried to live in harmony with his Boers. But we can't go on indefinitely in that manner. We are getting nowhere. If the government is in earnest, let it take the first steps!"

Pretoria

Otto gulped back his black coffee as Kruger inhaled, his pipe glowing brightly. Both men listened intently to Francois. From the stoep they could see the bonneted women and booted men, walking, riding and exchanging greetings while ox wagons rumbled past.

"So, there it is, Your Honour," Francois concluded. "The Uitlanders say it's they who have always offered the olive branch and you've rejected it. Now it's your turn."

"What's this about an olive branch?" Kruger interrupted, confused.

Francois smiled tactfully as he tried to explain. "Your Honour, in ancient Greece, the olive tree was the symbol of peace. So, to hold out a branch from that tree to an enemy means to make overtures for a truce. It's an act of friendship."

Kruger seemed more relaxed and took another puff of his pipe. "Good. Let's exchange these branches, by all means."

"The olive branch is also a symbol of fertility," interjected Otto. "Its leaves were worn as head-dress by brides in the hope that the marriage would be blessed with many children."

"*Bliksem*," Kruger exclaimed, quite alarmed. "That's quite another matter. There are too many Uitlanders already!"

Francois stifled laughter aggravated the situation as Kruger's dislike for the foreigners surfaced. Steely-eyed, he glowered, and his cheeks took on a red flush. "Go back to the people of Johannesburg. Tell them that we already offered the symbols of peace, the olive branch, as they call it, by withdrawing our police from the town to avoid conflict and reduce the possibility of civil war. It is for them to now say whether they will accept it."

A grin played over his serious expression. "But just be careful which olive branch you take with you, Mynheer du Plessis."

He turned away from Francois. That was his final word on the matter!

CHAPTER 14

Johannesburg

The town hummed with excitement; the prospect of the imminent overthrow of the Boers delighted the inhabitants. Jameson's progress was a source of constant speculation and his impending arrival a reality for all the assorted members of the population. Inside Hammond's office, however, the atmosphere was distinctly cool as he, Farrar and Phillips listened to Francois' reply.

"But we have no such confidence in the government. We mistrust the motives which inspired them to send you back here." Phillips replied, and the others murmured their approval.

"Whatever the government's attitude has been in the past, they are now genuinely anxious to remove the causes of discontent," Francois pointed out. "I believe you will get practically all you asked for in your Manifesto."

"What does that mean?" Hammond challenged him aggressively.

"Well, now," Francois' reply was diplomatic. "You cannot expect the government to come all the way along the road from Pretoria to meet you here in Johannesburg. You must go part of the way to meeting them." His eyes shifted from one to the other. "It's a matter of compromise."

"Is the government's change of heart and sudden reasonableness not because Dr Jameson is on his way to Jo'burg with a well-trained and well-equipped force?" Farrar quipped caustically.

Francois glanced at them and sensed mounting confrontation. Quietly he readdressed them and observed their reaction.

"Gentlemen, you are probably aware at this stage that the High Commissioner in Cape Town has issued a proclamation denouncing Dr Jameson's adventure. He has also called on him to return to British territory at once."

Their reaction was sudden and angry.

Hammond demanded," How do we know this isn't all just a trick of the government to gain time so that we can't join forces with Jameson?"

Hammond was the fuse, and Francois became aware of his burning antagonism and turned to face him. Their eyes locked defiantly.

"You are aware that since you have taken up arms and erected fortifications against the government and even, they believe, sent big guns out on the Pretoria road, they regard you as nothing but rebels."

They can call us what they like," Hammond scoffed. "All we want is justice, decent treatment and honest government."

An air of hostile silence was present.

"Will the people of Johannesburg consent to lay down their arms if the government grants most of what you ask?" Francois probed.

Phillips glanced over at the others for their approval, then responded. "Yes, certainly. I think I can say that after the enfranchisement, most of the new population will consider it a privilege to take up arms again as citizens of the Republic, should the need arise."

"On which lines do the Reform Committee propose the franchise should be granted?"

"We would be content, as a first step, if the government would accept the principle. The details could possibly be left to a commission of three, one representative on each side and the third to be mutually agreed upon," Phillips answered.

Francois nodded, then withdrawing a sheet of paper, he slowly unfolded it and handed it to Phillips. "Perhaps you would care to peruse and read this out loud for the benefit of your colleagues, Lionel. I think it is self-explanatory and represents the government's attitude to Johannesburg."

Phillips put on his spectacles and held the document up to the light as he began reading aloud. "The High Commissioner has offered his service with a view to a peaceful settlement. The Government of the South African Republic has accepted the offer. Pending his arrival, no retaliatory action will be taken against Johannesburg provided they take no hostile steps against the government."

He removed his glasses and thoughtfully deposited this document on the table, then gazed quizzically back at Francois. "May I enquire whether this offer from the government is intended to include Dr Jameson and his troops?"

"He falls into a different category. He's regarded as a foreign invader, and will be driven out of the country," Francois replied seriously.

Phillips sought the others' approval before he replied. "The delegation is not empowered to accept that which does not explicitly include Jameson. It's something which will have to be discussed with the entire Reform Committee and a reply sent to you as soon as possible."

"I think you gentlemen are suffering from a misapprehension. The Executives' resolution does not require an answer. If the people of Johannesburg observe the conditions, there will be no further trouble. Still, if they disregard them, they must bear full responsibility for all the consequences."

Pretoria

A few well-armed Boers in working clothes consisting of khaki pants, brown and dark green jerseys and bandoliers slung in a disorderly manner across their shoulders, halted in front of Kruger's stoep. Their leather saddles creaked in the afternoon's sunshine as their leader, General Otto dismounted and climbed the four wooden steps up onto the semi-open stoep. He was watched by both the still-mounted men and Paul Kruger who withdrew his pipe and let out a rasping cough, his Bible near at hand.

Otto's stout build cast a dark shadow over Kruger. As he approached, he held his floppy hat, respectfully in front of him. "Your Honour, we have come to greet you and at the same time to inform you that once we have captured Jameson, we intend to ride straight on to Johannesburg and shoot down that den of rebels there. They have provoked us long enough." His tone of voice matched the serious expression on his face.

Kruger drew pensively on his pipe, then calmly removed it, and placed it aside as he let his eyes focus on Otto. "No, *broeder*, you must not speak like that. Remember, there are thousands of innocent and loyal people in Johannesburg. The others have, for the most part, been misled." He leaned forward as he picked up his Bible.

Otto felt his cheeks flush as the rage within him surfaced. As usual, Kruger would try to use a biblical passage to justify his argument. "We must not be vengeful. Isn't there a text somewhere about forgiving our enemies?" Kruger asked.

"No, no, Mr President!" Otto interrupted, exasperated. "Don't turn to the New Testament, stick to the Old!"

The anger within Kruger mounted, yet outwardly he remained calm in the face of these hotheads. It was just that their timing was wrong. They thought they knew everything, but now they were likely to ruin it all.

"You, Mr President, you speak in vain," Otto pointed out. "What is the use of clemency? It is only because we have shown these rebels mercy for so long that they have gone so far. My men," he made a sweeping gesture towards his mounted riders, "and I are determined to end this sedition once and for all!"

Kruger slammed his Bible closed; his gruff voice matched his piercing, steely eyes. "Very well, if you will not listen to me, you can depose me from the presidency and govern the country after your own fashion."

Shaking his head slowly, Otto sighed in submission, his lips tightly drawn. "No, Mr President, I did not mean that. We are quite willing to listen to you, but we've been terribly provoked."

A pensive smile crossed Kruger's face fleetingly as he sensed Otto backing down. His own rage subsided. Yes, he might be an old bull, but he was still the leader of the herd. Otto was a good man even though he tended to let his anger control his head. "Well, if you will listen to me, do what I want and leave the rest to me. Remember there are two riders, but only one horse in the Transvaal. The question is which rider is going to sit in front, the Boers or the Uitlanders?"

Among the massed evergreens of the woods, there were bright spots of colour, careless dabs of nature's hand. Yellow, brown, orange and crimson, all vivid and distinct, grew in perfect harmony. Francois and Kate cantered through the veld. She glanced over at Francois who grinned back with a loving smile at her youthful exuberance.

A wildebeest dashed off in the distance, spurred on by the rhythmic beat of the horses' hooves. Summer was in the breeze and love was in the air as they galloped smoothly in tune with the free motion of their horses. In the distance, they saw the Boer commando, made up of young and even old men sporting shaggy white beards, although lacking any semblance of a uniform other than khaki. Their long Mauser rifles were attached to their saddles with two bandoliers slung around their shoulders and a small pouch to carry their biltong.

Kate called out a greeting as they neared. Wolf-whistles followed her as she passed. She giggled, then laughed out loud and glanced at Francois. He didn't see the funny side at all.

Reining in, Francois watched the commando disappear into the veld. A sinking feeling of obligation gripped him. Kate must have felt it too, for she asked, "Shouldn't you ride with them?"

He shrugged his shoulders as he watched the column of men moving away in the distance.

Kate sensed his dilemma and twisted in her saddle so that she could face him. "Well, Francois, what have you got to say?"

"I've been thinking about this whole saga," Francois finally answered. "Those people in Johannesburg have real grievances, but Jameson wasn't invited by them. Perhaps my place is to defend my *volk*."

Somehow, she had known it would come to this. Kate blew him a kiss as he wheeled his horse.

"Please, try to understand," Francois begged. She nodded, trying to hold back her tears. Then he slackened the reins and kneed his horse once in the ribs. "I'll come back to you, Kate, I promise!" he shouted and waved. Her sad eyes followed him as he left.

Cantering past the tethered horses, Francois entered the Boer encampment. No tents were visible. *They must be travelling light*, thought Francois as he picked his way among the men. An occasional Boer glanced up at him. The majority, however, were clustered around cooking fires, from which a strong smell of maize meal, boiling coffee and woodsmoke emanated. A flag fluttered in the breeze as he dismounted in front of the wagon.

Inside, General Otto sipped his black coffee and smacked his lips as he savoured the strong brew while writing a report.

"I want to join the commando!" Francois called out.

Puzzled, Otto looked up, then drew back the canvas folds and peered out, momentarily blinded by the sunlight. "Who's that out there?"

"It's Francois du Plessis, Piet." He grinned.

"Don't just stand there!" Otto exclaimed, and then beckoned him inside. "Pull up a *stoel* and join me for a *lekker koppie koffee*."

Now Francois knew he had made the right move.

Josh galloped on. He knew the implications of Rhodes' message. Jameson was coming, with or without their consent, and there was nothing that could be done.

Trying to take his mind off the immediate problem, he played spotting games with the springbok as they leapt gracefully out in front of him. Then, unbidden, his thoughts strayed back to Karina as the afternoon sun threw long spiderweb shadows across the veld. Her straight dark brown hair, so silky, her face smooth to his touch and those soft, warm breasts . . .

He recalled the feel of them against his chest. Had he done the right thing that night? Maybe he should have made love to her. Hell, he wanted her and could have had her. If he was a man, he would have loved her. Had she understood his rejection?

He felt confused and embarrassed. *Was it soft and warm down below*, he wondered? What colour was the hair there? He felt himself harden as the rhythmic motion of the horse jarred the saddle upward. It felt good yet strange. Was he enough of a man to show her just how much he wanted her?

In his reverie, with his tired eyes slightly closed and with the image of Karina dancing in his mind, he failed to see the Boer horsemen approaching. They surrounded him before he knew it.

The four Boers escorted him into camp. Josh was brought forward at gunpoint. Otto, seated among his men, glanced up at their captive.

They had taken a boy of no more than fifteen or sixteen. He barked at his men, instructing them to put their rifles away.

Josh watched him closely. General Otto was weather-beaten and wrinkled, with bright eyes and a long brown beard lightly grizzled.

"Where were you born?" he asked Josh harshly.

"In Bloemfontein," Josh lied.

"Being a Free Stater, your sympathy is with us." He was stern. "You are therefore commanded to take up a rifle in defence of the country."

"I have no grievance and don't believe you have a right to force me to take up arms," Josh retorted, acting somewhat braver than he felt. He was afraid that they would search him and find Rhodes' reply.

"Shoot him!" shouted elements of the hot-headed crowd closing in threateningly about him.

"No," Otto commanded gruffly, raising a restraining hand as he sensed their desire for blood. "Give him until sunrise tomorrow to decide. In the meantime, he must consider himself to be our prisoner."

Noticing the gathering crowd, Francois made his way over. Unable to see the central figure who was obscured by the men, he nudged a nearby Boer. "Who's the prisoner?"

"I hear he's a Free Stater," came the reply.

"What's he done?" Francois asked, intrigued.

"I don't know, but I hear he's to be shot in the morning."

Francois was still at the back of the crowd when the jostling started. Josh was grabbed by some of the younger hotheads and pushed towards the fire. His English accent still left them suspicious of his true identity. One youth aimed his rifle at Josh's head and squeezed the trigger. A dull thud echoed in Josh's terrified mind as the hammer made contact with the empty firing chamber. Lowering it, the youth inserted a cartridge shell into the breech, his eyes never leaving those of Josh. He smirked, then snapped the barrel shut. "This is for you tomorrow morning, perhaps even now, if you not careful." He placed his finger back on the trigger as Josh implored the others for help.

"What have I done?" Josh pleaded.

"You traitor!" replied the youth

"Coward!" another insult was hurled at him.

"You betray women and children!"

"*Engelse* lover," another spat out.

Francois threaded his way among them. Josh saw him with much relief. He had been granted a stay of execution. Francois moved towards the group of angry young men. "Leave him!" he shouted and walked right up to Josh.

The crowd parted. Francois put an arm around his shoulders and faced his tormentors. "Stop bothering him. I have known him and his pa for years, and you are to respect him while he is in our camp!"

Instantly their reaction changed; they greeted him as a brother, crowding around him. A mug of black coffee and *stuk* of biltong was thrust into his hands, and a blanket draped around his shoulders.

Later, when a hushed silence descended over the sleeping camp, Francois edged his way towards Josh, crawling on his elbows and knees. Around him, men lay stretched out, covered only by blankets, their heads resting on saddles as they slept. Two guards chatted amiably around the fire. Nobody spotted him.

Josh slept soundly, exhausted by the day's events. Francois placed a hand over his mouth and shook him. Instantly, Josh sat bolt upright, alarmed.

"Be still," Francois whispered. "All is well." The glow of the firelight threw darting shadows in the darkness as he handed Josh a sealed envelope.

"Listen, then act. Your life is in grave danger. This is an addressed envelope for the commandant of the police, Captain Malan. It's a fake letter, and you must destroy it on reaching Johannesburg. A horse will be tethered on the northern flank in an hour."

Francois took out a strip of white material from his pocket. "Tie this piece of rag around your right arm. Should you come across any patrols, they won't shoot you when they see this, but they'll want to know your mission. Show them the address on the envelope, and they'll allow you to pass." He paused, waiting for Josh to appreciate the gravity of the situation. "Understand, Josh, even though you and Kate are English, I'm still an Afrikaner, and I'm going to stop the Union Jack being illegally hoisted in the Republic." They clasped hands warmly before Francois blended back into the shadows.

Slowly, Josh edged his way out of the camp. He moved like he'd been taught to stalk game, keeping to the shadowy undergrowth. Snapping a twig with his foot, he paused, holding his breath, but no one stirred. Silently, he continued along behind the bushes, ant-heaps and trees. The ground was soft and sandy, already buzzing with insect life, and he moved easily enough without making much noise. Peering over the top of a scrubby bush, he searched the russet grass, then made his way over to the tethered horse. Unhobbling it, he led it quietly out into the first hint of the false dawn.

He was well clear of the camp before he dared mount. Then tying the cloth around his right arm, he disappeared, heading southward for Johannesburg.

CHAPTER 15

Johannesburg

The crowd milled angrily about the square, facing Hammond's office. His balcony was visibly devoid of any movement. Liquor flowed freely, as they grew louder with each new demand. Fists gesticulated in the air as the crowd became imbued with the prospect of a shift in the balance of political power. They anticipated the prospect of Jameson's victorious arrival.

The atmosphere grew explosive as the crowd edged closer to the building.

"What about Jameson?" Some of the diggers chanted.

"Yeah, what about him?" Rogaly called out from among the front ranks of the swelling crowd of men. Then he turned to face them and led them in a chant of "Jameson! Jameson!"

Inside the office, the Reformers glanced at each other. A loud cheer erupted as Phillips emerged onto the balcony with his hands held aloft for victory. Smiling, he gazed down at the expectant multitude.

"I'll tell you about Jameson if you give me a chance", he shouted.

A hushed silence enveloped the crowd as they waited for him to continue.

"The leader of the Reform Committee arranged for Jameson to assist us when and if it was required. Unfortunately, he has come before he was needed." An antagonistic murmur rippled through the mass as he again gestured for silence. "He has obviously acted on some false report that here, in Johannesburg, we were in danger and the Boers were in town killing and looting. So, he rushed to help us. For that, we must honour him. But of course, no such trouble was happening, or, as far as we know, is likely to happen. The reason we're now surrounded by armed commandos," he paused, "and why we've been repudiated by the British government, is because Jameson committed this act of war on a friendly state."

"Friendly to whom?" cried out Rogaly, precipitating further disenchanted rumblings among the diggers as Phillips tried to continue above their din.

"Don't let's forget that we're all in this together. We're on the same side with Dr Jameson." A mutter of assent riffled through the crowd as they hung onto his every word. "We, the committee, may regret his too hasty act in coming before we sent for him, but we're not going to let him down now. We must stand by him!"

Cheers filled the air. Relieved, Phillips quickly turned and faced the others who were watching him from within the office. He was smiling. Then he faced the crowd. "It is as a result of our efforts that the government has been persuaded to accept the offer of Her Majesty's High Commissioner to come to Pretoria and try to settle differences and avert bloodshed. An armistice has been agreed upon between us pending the arrival of Sir Hercules Robinson."

"What about Jameson?" Rogaly interjected loudly.

"Naturally, I cannot answer for him, but I know that the High Commissioner has ordered him to return to British territory. However, I am instructed by the Reform Committee to tell you positively that we intend to stand by Jameson."

The throng broke into spontaneous cheers as he continued. "Gentlemen, I now call upon you to give three cheers for Dr Jameson."

Down the main street through to the last staked claim, the cheering was audible as the excited crowd gave vent to their pent-up emotions.

General Otto silently moved his men into position. The morning sun beat down mercilessly as insects busied themselves, oblivious to the Boers creeping stealthily among the rocks high above the cliff face of the ravine at Doornkop. Far below, in a hollow at the base of the ravine, a few sharpshooters settled behind the craggy outcrop. Above, birds fluttered through the edges of the sky as rifles glinted in the sunlight. At the same time, more men swarmed upward rapidly working their way into a position as they sought the best vantage point.

Otto pointed the eyeglass in an easterly direction and peered at the dust bowl in the distance. He nodded, then passed the instrument on to Francois.

Although Jameson's men had cut the telegraph wires connecting Cape Town, they had failed to sever the telegraph wires to Pretoria.

"Lucky my men captured that drunk, MacLarty, near that telegraph pole. He cut the fence by mistake. Idiot. If he'd managed to cut the wire, we would not have been prepared for their moves! Stupid to get drunk." Francois nodded. "Finding him was a stroke of luck!"

Suddenly there was a rasping, squawking cry of a cockatoo. "Go away." An ugly, big-beaked go-away bird came sailing up from behind and flapped onto a nearby rock. They stood still for a few minutes giving it a chance to fly away, but it kept screeching and craning its neck at them. Picking up a stone, Francois threw it. The bird choked on a hysterical squawk of alarm and anger as the missile found its mark. Then it screamed even more noisily than before.

Two riders emerged simultaneously from the dust cloud, scouting ahead as Jameson's raiders made for the ravine. Otto acknowledged various signals from his men as they waited expectantly, the ambush ready.

"Piet, this is a sin; the Lord is looking at us." Francois shook his head ruefully.

"That's all right," replied Otto. "The Lord knows that this is the Boers' war, and, in wartime, He will always forgive a little foolishness like this." He signalled urgently to a group of Boers, still clearly visible, to take cover.

"If anything should happen to me, give this money to Kate, she's always asking for it." Francois took out a wad of notes and handed it to Otto.

Otto grinned and fumbled in his pocket. "*Ja*, and if I don't survive, give this arsenic to my brother, he's been wanting it too."

They chuckled, secure in their friendship as they gazed back down at the approaching raiders, confident that although they were outnumbered, their position was inaccessible to the enemy.

Just before entering the ravine's perimeter, and a short distance from the point of ambush, the scouts hesitated, speaking hurriedly to one another, then continued.

Otto glanced around at his men as they drew near with the two scouts still out in front, leading the procession. The Boers tensed, watching and waiting for Otto's signal at the head of the ravine. Carefully, both Otto and Francois levelled their rifles, their fingers on the triggers ready to fire as soon as they were within range.

A round of bullets rang out. The impact of the rifle's recoil jolted into Francois' shoulder as one of the scouts fell, kicking up the dry dust as he hit the ground. Immediately, the other drew on his reins, glanced up once in the Boers' direction, then dismounted and bent down over his wounded comrade. Raising him up, he lifted the wounded man across his saddle and taking the reins led the horse back on foot. Then, remembering, he turned and waved his acknowledgement up the ravine as Otto took aim once again. The scout was caught within his sights, and his finger tightened around the trigger.

Francois touched his shoulder. "Don't shoot, Piet. That's a brave man."

Otto hesitated, then lowered his rifle and cradled it under his arm. He waited, then gave the Boers the command to begin firing. A volley of bullets originated simultaneously from the entrenched positions as Jameson's' men dismounted and ran like disorganised ants in every direction, hunting and seeking any available cover. Bullets whined viciously around them, thudding and spewing up dust in their wake.

Spread out all around the base of the ravine, they vigorously returned the fire. Bullets now flew in every direction as the raiders began to fall.

The salvo was endless. One bullet hit a rock and ricocheted among Francois and his men, injuring one. Francois was shaken by the counterattack, and his bullets flew wide. Another group of raiders ducked among the bushes fringing the ravine and fired at random with their weapons, while one who was out in the open was shot in the face before he could take cover.

Johannesburg

"George!" Rogaly raced excitedly up to Farrar. "There's heavy firing coming from the direction of Krugersdorp. This is the moment, if we attack the rear of the Boer positions while Jameson's attacking the front, he'll be through."

"That's just why I sent for you," replied Farrar, officiously.

"How many men have you got mounted and armed?"

"Just over a hundred," Rogaly panted.

"Right! Take them out on the Krugersdorp road until you encounter the Boer positions. After that, act on your own initiative."

Rogaly spun around, ready to carry out Farrar's orders, but he was distracted by the galloping of a horseman. "There's somebody riding after us," he remarked puzzled.

Farrar raised his binoculars. "That's du Plessis' kid. Ten to one, he's been sent to stop us."

"Shall I shoot his bloody horse?" Rogaly asked, angrily.

"That's an idea," Farrar sniggered. "But we'd better not. Let's hear what he has to say."

"An order from the committee!" Josh shouted as he reared up and slid from his saddle. "A Boer attack is expected from the northwest. You've to take your men and patrol the area immediately!" Noticing Rogaly's silence, Josh added, "I was told to tell you that you are under the orders of the Reform Committee, and there is no question of disobeying them."

Disgruntled, Rogaly gave an angry gesture, spat on the ground, then turned and stormed off.

Meanwhile, many of the exposed horses were caught in the crossfire as the raiders cowered low behind the rocks, hardly daring to raise their heads as bullets continued to ricochet around them.

At last, the much-longed-for ammunition trolley rumbled upon the scene. A grey-haired man leapt up and handed down packets of cartridges. Just then, a Boer shell fell on to the ammunition trolley as the men dived for cover. For some inexplicable reason, it failed to explode.

Jameson regrouped a small cluster of men under an overhanging ledge, signalling to the others to fall back. The wounded, however, struggled to keep up. Noticing this, Jameson ordered them to the nearby barn from where they could surrender. At the same instant, his horse slipped away. Running after it, he caught hold of the bridle, then felt it slide from his grasp.

Instantly, the Boers appeared on his right flank, spurring him into renewed energy as he changed direction, feet flying, running after his men. Just then, one of his men arrived leading a dead soldier's horse. He threw the reins to Jameson who vaulted into the saddle, holding on desperately as the horse's momentum settled him on its back.

Moments later, to the Boer's surprise, another body of men rounded the point of the ravine. At full gallop, led by a Maxim gun drawn by four horses they seemed to fly over the ground, the horses' hooves thundering past the first line of men as they made straight for the hill.

Above, the Boers tried to shoot them, but they seemed to have coats of steel. The sharpshooters at the base of the ravine fired continuously, but to no avail, as they got to within 200 yards. Suddenly, one horse faltered, wounded, bringing the others to a standstill as bullets rained from above.

Briskly the men bravely hacked off the braces, severing them. The remaining three horses fled, riderless with their harnesses still intact. Risking their lives, the men loaded the Maxim gun. The very next instant, the automatic repeating weapon roared and rained bullets around the Boers, causing them to sink behind the boulders which hugged their shelter.

Scarcely lifting their heads because of the never-ending hail of bullets, they were oblivious to the field pieces brought into range a little to their left. Further shelling added to the continual, nerve-wracking bombardment. Silence, the Maxim gun ceased firing! Quickly, the Boer sharpshooters in the hollow took advantage and began firing back, while those on the hill joined in the general fusillade as metal whined, drowning out the occasional anguished cry of pain.

A body of horsemen raced into the midst of the Boer firepower. The Boers surprised, now desperately turned their fire as they tried to stop them. But to no purpose. Their pace did not falter. It appeared as if they would never stop. The Boer sharpshooters involuntarily fell back, overawed. Yelling and shouting like devils let loose, they came within twenty paces of the enemy. At that moment, as if by magic, they stopped and wheeled around at the sound of a trumpet. They returned at the same pace in the direction from which they came, leaving many wounded in the confusion.

General Otto, noting the whole of this force at the foot of the hill, shouted to his men to keep firing to engage the raider's attention. Silently, he despatched another body of men around the back of the hill and cut off any possible retreat. He and Francois watched them commence firing from the opposite direction. Now he had the raiders boxed in.

Otto snorted with a chuckle, "We have closed the gate of the *kraal* upon them, as it were. Just as the ox, finding itself caught, looks around to see if there's another gate it can escape from, so too is Jameson hunting for one. But all the avenues are barred!"

"Still, the raiders have fought bravely against such odds," Francois commented grudgingly. "Remember we're on the hill, and they're in the veld below."

Inside the farmhouse, men congregated enquiringly around Jameson, who peered dejectedly out of the window as he viewed clusters of men trapped behind rocks. He grimaced and turned back to his men as he shook his head, tears of terrible defeat welling up in his eyes.

One of the men attached a white shirt to the front end of his rifle. A feeling of desolation enveloped the room as he undid the latch. The window creaked open on its hinges. Slowly, he extended the rifle. The shirt fluttered in full view of those perched high up on the ravine.

"There goes my life," Jameson muttered, his hair ruffled. His bloodshot eyes matched his pale, drawn face as he heard the Boer Commander order his men to stop firing. The sudden deafening lull from the battlefield endorsed his sense of defeat. "We surrender," he shouted. "Provided you guarantee safe conduct out of the country for every member of the force."

A cheer rose and swelled around the peaks into a crescendo as the entrenched, triumphant Boers gave vent to their emotions. "If you undertake to pay the expenses which you have caused the Zuid-Afrikaanse Republiek and will give up your flag and your arms, I will spare the lives of you and your men." Otto shouted, his voice carrying down the ravine.

Otto and Francois wound their way down the mountain to much cheering, as Jameson's men filed forlornly out of the farmhouse. The raiders looked a sorry crowd, dirty, miserable, sixteen dead, many of them seriously wounded, some weeping and Jameson shaking like a leaf in the wind.

Making their way through Jameson's still armed and hostile force, they dismounted and headed for the farmhouse as Jameson emerged into the sunlight ignoring Otto's outstretched hand.

Shrugging off Jameson's snub, Otto smiled as he stood there. He was triumphant, his opponent bitter in defeat. "Dr Jameson, it is an honour to finally meet you." Otto couldn't fail to hide his triumphant tone of voice. "I understand that you and your men will surrender yourselves with your flag and everything you possess?"

I have no flag," Jameson replied curtly.

Otto gazed in disbelief at Jameson, then at Francois and finally back at Jameson again. "Will you swear to that under oath?"

"I declare upon my oath that I have no flag." Jameson answer was bland.

Otto raised his eyebrows. "Then I must believe your word."

Cape Town

Rhodes paced the floor of his office, his mind reeling. Jameson had indeed upset his applecart. For twenty years, they'd been friends. Now his ally had ruined him. There was no course open to him, but to hand in his resignation. He imagined how the conversation with the High Commissioner would develop.

"Tell me it's not true. Tell me you didn't direct Jameson to proceed," the High Commissioner would insist.

"How can I say that? Jameson is an old friend of mine, I can't let him down," he would respond.

The High Commissioner would become more persuasive, his voice pleading. "Then, you must issue a proclamation repudiating Jameson's raid and dismiss him as Administrator for Rhodesia."

Rhodes would grow silent, then possibly stammer as he raised his hand to explain. *How could he expect him to take that action? Jameson was his friend.* Then nodding knowingly, the High Commissioner would respond. "I see now. I understand. You don't need to say anything more."

Now Rhodes passed a hand over his bleary eyes as he muttered to himself. *Now that I'm down, I shall see who my real friends are.*

He paused, then picked up his fountain pen and related the events to the High Commissioner, then added. "You must proceed to Johannesburg to salvage the situation. Once there, you must ensure that you receive a splendid reception and turn the position to England's advantage. My resignation will be forwarded to you immediately."

His shoulders drooped as he shook his head sadly; *So little done, so much still to do* . . .

CHAPTER 16

Johannesburg

The mob that gathered in the square was angry. Inside the office, Farrar, Phillips and Hammond confronted the stone-faced General Otto and an equally stern Francois du Plessis. Kate hovered in the background, pen and notepaper at hand.

"Jameson! Jameson! We want arms for his rescue," chanted the masses outside.

One of the Reformers burst into the room. The door echoed as it slammed, striking the wood panelling behind it. The man was breathless. "There are a number of men in front of that crowd who are planning to blow up this building. We can hear them quite plainly. They've already sent off for some cases of dynamite!"

Thanks." Phillips looked stern. "Please keep us informed of any new developments." Then he turned to face Otto and Francois. "Well now, gentlemen, it's no use asking my chaps to take on that lot outside. We've got to use reason and persuasion, not force. If that crowd gets out of hand, they'll tear the town apart and us with it."

"What do you suggest then, Lionel?" Hammond asked.

"Well, you'd better try some effective speechmaking from the balcony, for a start."

"Good idea," Farrar interrupted, moving rapidly across the room past the oak panel towards the closed glass doors. "I know these men out there, and they know me. I'll have a go."

Opening the doors wide, he stepped out onto the balcony. Before him, people teemed angrily, shouting among themselves. Immediately he was greeted by a howl of abuse from the enraged mob.

He stepped back into the office. Phillips walked briskly past him brushing him aside. He gripped the railing tightly. In vain, he tried to make his voice heard over the noise of the crowd.

"We want Jameson, we want Jameson!" they continued to chant in unison. Phillips also withdrew.

Kate hesitated for a moment, then ventured out alone onto the now-empty balcony. She waved to them and called out to the ones she knew by name. Slowly their chanting subsided.

"My father is eighty-four," she shouted. "But if I surrender, he'll shoot me for cowardice!"

A cry of agreement echoed back as the crowd warmed to her, latching on to each word. "Gentlemen, I beg you for Jameson's sake, do maintain a spirit of calm and restraint. I assure you that the Reform Committee has done everything in its power for him. This will be recognised when all the facts are known. Jameson's life may be in grave danger. By your actions tonight and in the days to come, you may decide his future and that of all the brave men who followed him from Pitsani."

She paused, waiting for the implications of what she said to sink in before continuing. "Now I want you to listen to General Otto, who has come from Pretoria to speak to you."

A hushed murmur spread around the crowd as Otto approached the balcony. Gruffly, he commenced, his stern eyes taking in the mood of those below him. "As most of you know, I am the representative for the Boer government, and you can accept, therefore, that I have nothing but the best interests of Johannesburg and its people at heart. It is because of that, that I tell you this morning to lay down your arms."

He hesitated, waiting for them to settle. He sensed their antagonism, still ... there was no movement so he adopted a more authoritative and threatening attitude, "I feel my duty is to point out to you that you will be exposing the town and all its inhabitants, including the women and children, to the gravest risks if you do not comply." He paused as he waited for the ripple of disapproval to die down. "I must warn you that Johannesburg is defenceless."

"What do you mean by that?" A digger called from among the front ranks.

"We not afraid of a bunch of backveld farmers!" howled another. "Go back to Pretoria. And tell Paul Kruger to come and get our rifles if he can." He held his weapon aloft to the cheers of the mob as they pressed forward, jeering comments flying thick and fast.

Inside the office, Hammond turned to the others. "The damn old fool! He thinks he can frighten them into giving up their arms. We've got to stop him before they start moving to Pretoria. Francois, will you say something to them? Jameson's life may depend on the mob. Try to make them see reason. Appeal to them. And George, get Otto off that balcony. Pull him by the scruff of his neck if you have to."

Farrar slipped onto the balcony and whispered into Otto's ear. Bewildered, Otto shook his head vigorously. Grabbing hold of his elbow, Farrar dragged him off the balcony to the derisive jeers and laughter of the mob. Emerging grim-faced out onto the balcony, Francois held up both arms for quiet. There was silence.

"Men and women of Johannesburg," he began loudly, his voice carrying over the crowd. "As your member of the Volksraad, you must know that I sympathise deeply with you in your struggle for what I believe to be your rights." An undertone of agreement emanated from the townsfolk. "There is no need for me to remind you that Jameson and his men are prisoners in Pretoria, but perhaps you need to recall that their lives are in grave danger. They are, in fact, hostages for your good behaviour. I know what you'd like to do. You want to march straight from here to the Boer capital. It may be that you'll reach it, though I would not rate your chances very highly."

Grinning, he held up his hands to stem the tide of dissenting shouts. "All right! You'll reach Pretoria, but what do you think you'll find there, huh? Jameson and his followers lined up to cheer you in? I tell you that you'll only find their corpses! The Boer government has made one condition for their safety, only one! You must give up your arms! It is not surrendering. You will be delivering them to the Reform Committee. And in return, Jameson and his men will be delivered. As well as those who have led their movement, and who, let me assure you, are in no way responsible for this unfortunate ending. No, not it's ending, for I do not believe that it will end until it has achieved its objectives."

He paused. "And so, my friends, I, whose heart and soul are with you, I say again, give up your arms to your Reform Committee. You'll be surrendering nothing of value. This city you've built should grow on in greatness and prosperity. Give up your arms and go back to your work and your homes. You will never regret it!"

A moment of indecision precipitated any movement, then slowly they shuffled forward and handed in their arms. A smile flitted across Francois' face as he watched them. The crowd thinned as small groups drifted away down the road.

Outside the Heights Hotel, a Boer announced the proclamation before affixing it to a prominent tree trunk. Inside, a shocked silence of disbelief spread over those present as the crier's voice filtered through the open windows.

"I, Stephanus Paulus Kruger, proclaim that all persons and corporations who are the chief offenders, ringleaders, leaders, instigators and those who caused the rebellion of Johannesburg shall answer for their deeds before the legal and competent courts of the Republic."

"The cunning old bastard," Farrar blurted out. "First he gets us to disarm, then he waits two days while he moves his blasted commandos and Zarps into position, then he issues this. You know what it is? It's not a proclamation at all but a bloody warrant for our arrest!"

"I don't believe the authorities in Pretoria will dare put us in jail." Phillips interrupted. "Not after giving their recognition to the committee."

"After all, they've accepted us as negotiators on behalf of all the people of Jo'burg." Hammond added. "Besides, Great Britain would never allow any harm to befall her subjects after commanding them to lay down their arms and guaranteeing their safety."

"But, you're not British, John," Phillips reminded him grimly.

"Well, nobody's gonna make an exception for me just 'cause I'm an American. We've got a government too, you know."

The Reader's voice droned on as he reeled off names, ". . ., George Farrar, Frank Rhodes, Percy FitzPatrick, John Hays Hammond, Lionel Phillips, . . ." The people in the room froze as the gravity of the situation was understood. Outside, horses' hooves clattered in the courtyard.

"That'll be the Zarps," Hammond commented dryly. "They'll be up here soon. I think we'd better start getting a few things ready. Then we'll meet back here for a last drink."

Otto dismounted, then signalled to his men to remain in position as he walked on to the hotel stoep flanked by two of his men. He pulled the chord; the bell echoed loudly deep inside the hallway. Slowly the heavy oak door creaked open as Rogaly gazed at them and sneered, "Hello, General! Nice evening." He smiled up at the star-studded sky, but his eyes remained cold and despising.

"Not so pleasant as you might think, Mynheer Rogaly," he answered in an acerbic tone. "Do you mind if we come in?"

Rogaly adopted a belligerent attitude. "Since when were you a member, General?"

"These are the names of some people we would like to see, and these are the warrants for their arrest," Otto replied angrily, as he waved the documents in Rogaly's face. "We believe that they are here now."

Otto took two steps forward in the direction of the doorway, but Rogaly remained impassive and blocked his way. His cold hatred flared as he struggled to control his temper and his fists. "I'm sorry, General. This is a private hotel. You can only enter if you're a member or at a member's invitation. I, for one, won't be inviting you in. Them's the rules, and I have to obey them."

"Rogaly, you cheeky rooinek." Otto's nostrils flared. "This warrant gives us the right to enter and search the premises. If you don't get out of the way damn quickly, you'll also be arrested. Now, move!"

Rogaly still refused to be intimidated. Instead, he savoured his opportunity of matching wits. "Tell you what, General, come in and sit down; I think this is a matter for the Chairman. I'll send for him." He smirked as he stood aside and allowed Otto and his men to enter.

Calling Josh over towards a corner, Rogaly whispered urgently into his ear. "Get hold of Mister Hammond and the others and tell them that the Zarps and General Otto are here to arrest the entire Reform Committee. They must get the hell out of here by the back door."

"Rather tell them that the place is surrounded. Escape is impossible." Otto eavesdropping spun on his heels as he faced Rogaly.

He shrugged his shoulders in resignation. "Just go to the billiard room and card room, boy, and let them know that the Zarps have come for them."

A surprising jocular crowd soon jammed the hallway and insisted on being arrested as the word spread. Lionel Phillips elbowed his way through the throng and greeted Otto jovially. "Just a minute, General. Surely, we've got time for a nightcap. It may be a long time before we can get another one. Why don't you join us?"

Otto replied gruffly. "You can have ten minutes," he relented, then added, "And if I were you, I wouldn't just drink. The arrangements up at the jail are not very satisfactory."

Drawing Rogaly aside, Phillips thrust a thick wad of notes into his hand. "You can bribe these Boers to do anything. A soon as you find out what's happening to us, see that we're well supplied with food and drink." He chuckled. "No champagne unless you can get some ice to go with it. And Rogaly, we'll need some cricket gear, pads and two or three balls. Let's pray it won't be necessary for you to bring some footballs."

In the Johannesburg Volksraad office, the dull yellow glow of an oil lamp provided some light as Francois busied himself with neglected paperwork. Outside everything remained subdued. Behind him, the Reformers' files were stacked neatly in piles.

The sound of footsteps suddenly echoed through the tiny office, causing Francois to lose his concentration as he glanced up. A smile creased his face as he saw Otto and his assistant standing in the doorway, with a hessian sack in Otto's hand.

"Hello, Piet," he exclaimed, moving round to the other side of the desk. "Nice to see you back on duty again. What can I do for you?"

Otto rummaged through his pockets and drew out a document. "Francois du Plessis, I have a warrant for your arrest!"

Francois blinked, taken aback. "Well, I can't say that I'm altogether astonished, but you'd better let me see it. We Raad members have got to observe all the formalities, eh?" He smiled weakly before taking hold of the document, but not before Otto seemed to hesitate and point to something.

He scanned it for a moment in silence. Otto's assistant watched carefully, before he commented wryly, "Well, Piet, it seems to be in order." Then he frowned, "Wait a minute! January 10th. Today is the ninth. Somebody's made a mistake, or you're both two hours early. Look for yourself!"

A smile curled around the edges of Otto's mouth, and his eyes twinkled. He casually scratched his bushy beard. "That's right enough, Francois. What the hell do I do now?"

Francois understood his meaning. He pointed to the other room. "Well, you can make yourself comfortable next door for a couple of hours. You'll find a couch in there, and a drink in the cupboard. Make yourself at home."

"That's very kind of you, Francois," Otto replied, still smiling. "But I think I'd better go back to the office and get this put right. If they've made the same mistake on all the warrants–" His voice trailed off as he waved his hand and shrugged his shoulders.

"I hadn't thought of that. Yes, that's what you'd better do, Piet. I'll get on with my work in the meantime. Got a lot still to do. See you later, Piet."

"Yes, I'll be back soon," Otto replied, casually dropping the sack, then turned towards the doorway, where he stopped and raised his voice. "Don't you try to get away, Francois. My men are posted all around the building."

"Now, why would I want to escape?" Francois asked.

"Because they're going to make an example of you by having you, an Afrikaner, shot for supporting the Uitlanders!" His voice carried to his men outside. He banged the door behind him.

Intrigued, Francois eyed the sack that Otto had dropped. He bent down and untied the knot, then peered inside. Surprised, he withdrew a false white beard, some white powder, a slouch hat and an overcoat. He smiled at his friend's insinuation and gazed across at the window. Moving quickly towards it, he closed the curtain.

Outside a group of dismounted Zarps huddled around a small crackling fire. Their horses grazed handily nearby. Francois put on the disguise of a bearded old Boer. He threw some white powder over his hair, then examined himself in the mirror before placing the hat on his head.

The disguise was perfect.

Leaving the lamp burning, he silently slipped out the front door, keeping well back in the shadows for the first few paces. He patted his two revolvers in the pockets of the overcoat and felt reassured by the steel of two bayonets beneath his belt. He drew in his breath, slouched and rounded his shoulders, then walked boldly over to the huddled Zarps. He threw them with his sudden appearance as he patted their horses and spoke in their language. "That looks like a fine animal. Will you sell him?"

"If it was mine, I would." The guard was friendly. "But it belongs to the government, so I can't."

"*Ja wel*, the government." Francois reply was gruff. "All the best things belong to them, except for the gold mines. If they owned those, then we could all have horses like these for nothing."

The Zarps considered the idea, then shrugged their shoulders. "Perhaps they will take over the gold mines when all this trouble is over."

"Then you'll get your own horses." Francois gave a throaty chuckle and walked off into the night, leaving the unsuspecting guards still huddled around the fire.

CHAPTER 17

Pretoria

A few days after the raid, the Kaiser of Germany sent a telegram congratulating President Kruger and the Transvaal government on their success "without the help of friendly powers", alluding to the possible support from Germany. When this was disclosed in the British press, it raised a storm of anti-German feeling. Meanwhile, Dr Jameson was lionised by the press and London society, now inflamed by anti-Boer and anti-German feeling and in a frenzy of jingoism.

Kruger was never more popular and jollier than he had been in years. He had protested to the British Colonial Secretary, Joseph Chamberlain in no uncertain terms, accusing the British government of involvement. He knew Chamberlain was behind Rhodes prompting the invasion, even though Chamberlain did his best to keep his name out of the newspapers. He surmised that this was the opening salvo in England's attempt, backed by America, to keep this part of Africa "English speaking", and take over the gold and diamond fields before any other powerful political rivals.

At the same time, Kruger ignored talk of the death penalty for the imprisoned Jameson or a campaign of retribution against Johannesburg, challenging his more bellicose commandants to depose him if they disagreed. However, he now wore the knightly orders, newly conferred upon him by the Netherlands, Portugal, Belgium and France on his sash of state.

After confiscating the weapons and munitions stockpiled by the Reform Committee, as urged by Chamberlain, Kruger handed Jameson and his troops over to the British government to be returned to England for trial. He granted amnesty to all the Johannesburg conspirators except for sixty-four leading members, who were charged with high treason, and thrown into jail in Pretoria.

Kruger's handling of the affair made his name a household word across the world. Also, it won him abundant support from Afrikaners in the Cape and the Orange Free State and other dignitaries, who began visiting Pretoria in large numbers.

Kate walked onto the stoep, where Paul Kruger sat. He greeted her with an outstretched hand.

"I haven't come to talk politics," she assured him as he beckoned her to be seated. At first, the idea of going to see the President terrified her. The deep voice that rumbled like a volcano, then the flecked beard that rimmed his face, bushy eyebrows, and that tight-fitting black frocked coat—all inspired awe. Her heart pounded wildly, and her breathing was rapid, but he never hurried her. She felt a feeling of warmth and respect emanating from him.

"No, not politics," he replied in English as he filled his pipe from a moleskin pouch, still uncertain of the reason for attractive woman's presence.

"Nor have I come to ask a favour for the Reformers, as I'm sure the honesty of their motives will speak for themselves on the day of the trial. I come as a woman and daughter of the Republic to ask you to continue the clemency that you have thus far shown and thank Mrs Kruger for the tears she shed when Johannesburg was imperilled."

Kruger relaxed visibly. He leaned forward slowly and picked up his pipe, knocking it against the side of the table, then drew on it thoughtfully. "That is true, she did weep. Where were you?" he asked quizzically as he peered at her knowingly.

"I was in Johannesburg with Francois before he helped capture Jameson."

As Kruger drew on his pipe again, the smoke with its pungent sweet smell rose idly. "Were you not afraid?"

"Yes," she reflected. "Those days have robbed me of my youth."

He gave a brief smile. "And what did you think I was going to do?"

"I hoped that you would come to an understanding with the Reformers," Kate replied boldly.

Kruger contemplated her answer. "I was disappointed that the English went against me," he growled.

"You must come to England, Mr President, as soon as all this trouble is settled, and see how we manage matters."

Kruger's face lit up with interest. "I'm too old to go so far," he replied pensively.

She smiled, and her eyes twinkled. "No man is older than his brain, Mr President."

Kruger chuckled to himself, and then removed the pipe from between his teeth. He coughed raucously then rose and extended his hand. "I shall be glad to serve you in any way possible."

"Then will you tell your good wife that I am praying to the same God that peace may come."

The elderly statesman watched the young woman walk down the road. What a pity they were on opposing sides.

Pretoria

The wrought iron gate slammed shut behind her as she threaded her way past the armed guards into the jail courtyard. The Reformers mustered around Kate excitedly.

"How did you ever find your way into this Godforsaken hole?" enquired Hammond.

"Getting into jail is easy," Kate bantered. "I thought the difficulty arose when it came to getting out. I hear you're going to stand trial soon."

"The Boers can't get away with this," Farrar interjected.

"Like hell they can't! They're doing it, aren't they?" replied Kate, suddenly angry at their short-sightedness.

"Pluck, it's pluck, that's wanted," Phillips retorted, adopting a patriotic attitude somehow out of touch with the reality they faced.

"You have it, for you've plucked everybody I know. You know what I admire about you?" Kate added, shaking her head sadly. "You're always English. England treats you like dirt. She's only interested in you when she can reap what you've sown, but she ignores you when you get into trouble." She paused as she nodded, considering what she said, then gave a mischievous grin. "Hell, if I had command of the campaign, I would have moved secretly by night to a point nearby a Boer camp. There I would build a pyramid of biltong and Bibles 50 feet high and send word to their spies, and then, when the rest came with a rush, I would have surrounded them."

They all chuckled at the perceived stupidity and naivete of the Boers.

"Incidentally, John," Kate added, "The United States Secretary of State, Mister Olney, sent a telegram saying, 'Take instant measures to protect John Hays Hammond and see that he has fair play.'" She smiled as she watched his reaction. "I thought you'd be pleased to hear that. I've also received a letter from Rhodes." She unfolded the paper and read its contents. "I can scarcely tell you how sorry I feel for you. I am writing a line to say that you must keep up your hope. Things will turn out much better than you think." Her voice trailed off.

Hammond's comment was dry and bitter. "The right one, sitting there in Cape Town at the seaside, far away from the firing line".

"By the way, Kate," Phillips interjected, placing a fatherly arm around her shoulders. "We are sorry about Francois. It seems so unfair. He only did what he thought was right and honest. We always respected him for that."

Her tone became sad. "Yes, although I cannot think of him as an Afrikaner, his father and grandfather were farmers. He felt it his duty to fight with the Boers. He bore no enmity to anyone. I really don't think poor Francois knew what he was fighting for."

Suddenly, Hammond hammered his fist into the wall. "It was all so unnecessary! That's what frustrates me. Jameson took it on himself to attack although his force was hopelessly outnumbered."

"But surely Jameson expected to go forward?" Kate asked puzzled.

"No, he wasn't strong enough. The idea was that he should wait where he was."

A gloomy silence enveloped them. Then Kate tried to lift the gloom and put on a cheerful front. "So, boys, how are you going to plead?"

"We've decided to plead guilty," Hammond replied suddenly serious.

"Guilty of high treason?" she gasped.

"I'm afraid so, my dear," Phillips stated. "We thought all along that the government had no evidence against us. Our council has been informed that they have taken not only Jameson's papers but all our correspondence from John's desk."

"But you can't plead guilty, Lionel!" Kate wailed. "They'll hang or shoot you."

Phillips shook his head, smiling benignly as he rested his arm reassuringly about her waist and led her away from the others. "It's not as bad as that, my dear. What I tell you now is in absolute confidence. You mustn't breathe a word to anyone, otherwise, we'll end up with a noose around our necks."

He kissed her gently on the cheek. "Now listen carefully, Kate, and you'll understand our predicament." He lowered the tone of his voice. "There are four indictments. The first concerns the invitation to Dr Jameson to invade the Transvaal. The second accuses us of inciting the people of Johannesburg to assist us. The third relates to the distribution of arms and ammunition. Lastly, there's a charge of forming and arming our police force."

"But don't you see," Kate interrupted. "If you plead guilty–"

"Wait till I've finished, my dear, then I think you'll understand. We're faced with three options. We can plead not guilty to all the charges and enter a long-drawn-out trial before a hostile judge and jury. There, every statement in our defence would be regarded as another attack on the state. The second choice would be to refuse to plead at all, and the third is to plead guilty and take a short cut on the best terms we can get to what is virtually a pre-arranged conclusion."

Kate's eyes widened with a look of confusion. "What do you mean by that?"

"That's what we've been discussing. Our council and Otto have had a meeting. Otto has made an offer. If we," he gave a sharp intake of breath, "If we plead guilty to the first indictment, they'll withdraw counts two, three and four. After very careful consideration, it seems that a plea of guilty would be best for all concerned. There's also the fact that in doing so, we would not be incriminating Dr Jameson, who has still to be tried in England."

Kate stared back incredulously at him, then over at the others. "Why should you worry about Jameson? He and his officers have done nothing but incriminate you from the moment the affair started. Don't do it, Lionel! It's just another trap for you. Just like the one you've walked into before."

The tears welled up, trickling gently down her cheeks as she turned and made her way back towards the prison gate. Phillips hesitated, then dashed after her. He stopped her, and then tried to console her. Her wet eyes beseeched him as she shook her head from side to side. "Don't you see, Lionel?" They intended to hang you all."

Kate could taste the dry film of dust particles hanging in the afternoon sunlight as she swept the floor. It was always dusty ever since the mining started. Disfiguring the landscape, denuding foliage and trees, leaving behind mountains of disused loose earth piled into hillocks as diggers searched deeper and deeper for gold.

Daydreaming, she was lost in thought. *Where was Francois hiding? Who was there to help him? He hadn't done anything wrong, yet they were hunting for him. He had all along acted in a manner he thought was right and honourable. And now where had it landed him.*

Without warning the door swung open. Kate caught her breath. Spangled in the shards of sunlight stood Francois, unshaven and dirty, yet grinning as he spied Kate. She rushed over to him, burying her head in his chest as his arms enveloped her, hugging her closer.

"I'm sorry I couldn't tell you," he whispered. "There just wasn't time."

She made some tea from the red bush tree-leaves while he explained what had happened, and how General Otto had helped. He was a gruff but fair man, and although he had a job to do, he knew right from wrong.

Francois continued as he sipped his tea. "I can't run, Kate. I must give myself up! I never did anything wrong. All I was trying to do was represent Jo'burg and get the reforms, which was why I was elected. I have to clear my name and help the others. Kruger will see the light once the emotions have calmed down."

He was right, but she didn't want to lose him. How had they got into this mess? Confused, all she knew was that she loved him and would always stand by him whatever he decided. All she wanted to do was hold him as she moved closer, seating herself on his lap, cuddling closer.

Smiling, he caressed her breasts, squeezing the nipples playfully as they hardened to his touch, protruding through her cotton dress. They were his to feel, warm and soft, as he drew her closer. He nibbled at her ear, then gently caressed her neck, kissing her, sending a tingle down her spine.

"I love you, Katy," he whispered as he kissed her longingly, holding her tongue with his.

Drawing back breathlessly, she gazed at him with adoration. "I love you too, my darling."

There was no urgency, only the knowledge of total loyalty and love as they slowly undressed. The warmth of their bodies merging as their limbs intertwined like satin, exploring each other with their touch in ways they would never do with anyone else. After a while, they were ready as Francois slid into her warm, glistening juices. She gave a little sigh, then he planted his seed.

Pretoria

The newly built Market Hall with its Dutch architecture and gabled roof bearing the inscription of the year 1887 above the doorway would have passed for a typical Dutch homestead. Today, the atmosphere was festive as the Pretoria townsfolk strolled in and out of the courtroom, leaving their black *piccanin* boys outside to tend to their wagons.

Boers vied for seats on either side of the dock and witness box as they entered the courtroom. The bonneted women in long dresses, covering layers of petticoats, bore baskets carrying *koeksusters* and *melkterts*.

The latter they handed around to their menfolk who were resplendent in floppy pants, clean shirts and felt hats. Some of the men had removed their headgear out of respect and laid them on their laps.

The Johannesburg Uitlanders were going to get their just desserts. Particularly now that Polish Judge Reinhold Gregorowski had been summoned from among their Boer brothers in the neighbouring Republic of the Free State to try these gangsters.

He was invited to preside over the trial of the Reform prisoners at Pretoria despite having no status to practice law nor sit on the bench in the Transvaal. Noted for the peculiar severity of his sentences of all except Boers, he arrived intending to stretch the law as severely as possible against the prisoners.

The frivolity increased as greetings echoed around the courtroom. Men and women now filled the doorways and spilled over outside. The latecomers would be forced to peer through the windows.

The church bells tolled as the prisoners were led up into the dock. They were greeted by a howl of abusive insults which stilled as soon as Judge Gregorowski entered the courtroom. The onlookers rose and waited for the learned judge to take his seat on the bench before they sat down. With the bang of his gavel, the trial commenced.

Just as the first witness was called, there was a sudden and fearful noise. The courtroom was filled with thick dust. A poorly hung oil lamp clattered to the floor. Immediately Gregorowski dashed from his elevated chair through his private chambers, his black coat flapping behind him, and into the square outside. A great cloud of dust in the shape of an open parachute hung over the town. Some anarchist had detonated a mass of explosive. Would this unlawful act prevent the trial from proceeding?

The judge returned, having decided to carry on. After all, he had a job to do. The trial had to resume. He banged his gavel again. Quiet suddenly reigned through the tumult of questions. The court was in session.

Phillips glanced through a newspaper in the courtroom, apparently unconcerned while the Reformers' brilliant young advocate, J.W. Wessels, continued his cross-examination of General Otto. "You said you were present when the Johannesburg deputation met the President."

"*Ja*," Otto answered carefully. "But if you're going to ask me about anything that took place at that meeting, I cannot answer because the meeting was a privileged one."

The Boers in the courtroom chuckled as Wessels was forced to try another approach. Now, he paced about in front of the witness box, with his hands clasped firmly behind his back. Halting, he passed a hand over his brow as if in thought. "You have stated that you were once a Landdrost."

"*Ja*," Otto replied.

An incredulous expression swept over Wessels' face. "And you tell me that you feel free to divulge as much as it suits the government to reveal, but that as soon as I wish to prove something to my clients' advantage, the interview suddenly becomes privileged?"

Otto stared back at the defence counsel, sullen and silent. Exasperated, Wessels turned to the bench. "I appeal to you, Your Honour, to direct this witness to answer my question."

The public gallery waited with bated breath for the Judge's directive. The bewigged jurist admonished Wessels. "Witness's contention upheld."

The Boers hooted their approval and laughed at Wessels' discomfort. Suddenly heads swung round as their attention was drawn to a slight commotion in the doorway. Barney Barnato pushed past the crowded onlookers. As he strode into the courtroom, he greeted those in the gallery whom he knew. Cheers emanated from the small group of Uitlanders, and the prisoners smiled in welcome at their ally.

"Barney, when did you arrive?" Kate asked as he took a seat alongside her. She smiled, relieved at his arrival.

"Just got back! I took the first steamer out of Europe as soon as I heard about the raid." He beamed and nodded at the judge to proceed. "Don't worry, Kate," he whispered. "I'll get them out, mark my words." He glanced around him. "Why isn't Rogaly being charged with the four?"

"They regard him as only a clerk," Kate spoke in a low voice as Gregorowski hammered the gavel for silence. Barnato glared at the judge. "And why, Gregorowski?" He did not lower the tone of his voice this time.

"They imported him from the Free State because none of the judges here were prepared to try their case!"

Barnato said nothing. All he did was nod. From this moment on, he would listen to every word, and, if need be, play an active role in his friends' defence.

CHAPTER 18

The toll of a church bell announced that the trial had recommenced. General Piet Otto emerged from those among the prosecution bench. He handed a letter to the judge as he addressed both Gregorowski and the courtroom. "This letter was found in Dr Jameson's possession when he was captured."

"Did he make any attempt to conceal or destroy it?" Gregorowski enquired, while he perused its contents.

"On the contrary, Your Honour. I may say that the State Attorney's Department has made every effort to obtain the original letter without success. I have reason to believe it is in England. Dr Jameson has certified that this is a true copy."

"Are you certain?" Wessels interjected and rose to his feet.

"Ja," Otto replied defiantly.

"How do you know?" Wessels queried, a gleam in his eyes.

"Because it is certified," Otto responded, stabbing the document with his forefinger. The public gallery followed the confrontation enthusiastically.

"Did you see the original?"

"*Nee.*" Otto shook his head, trying to figure out the object of this line of questioning.

"Then the only reason you have in stating that this is a true copy is that Jameson told you so?" Wessels raised his eyebrows and spread his hands in a threatening gesture.

"That's correct."

"Thus," Wessels said, turning to face both judge and the courtroom. "If I were to go and write the greatest nonsense in the world and sign it, then inform you that it is a correct copy of a certain letter, would you come and swear so?"

"Nee!" Otto retorted angrily, trying to counter the insinuation.

"As a matter of fact," Wessels added, turning upon Otto and verbally attacking him. "All you know is that Jameson told you that the document was a copy of the original letter. Can you guarantee the contents?"

"Do you dispute the accuracy of the copy, *Advokaat* Wessels?" Gregorowski enquired, frowning as he interrupted the defence council's momentum.

"No, Your Honour," Wessels replied in a respectful tone. "We do not dispute the accuracy, but it is absolutely certain that the original document did not contain a date, nor all these signatures. This has a date, and there are one or two other discrepancies—so we cannot admit it."

Gregorowski smiled as he relaxed back into his chair. "The letter will be admitted, but the court will bear in mind what you have said regarding the date. However, the signatures are irrelevant. It is a question, Advokaat, of intent and knowledge rather than time."

Francois smirked sarcastically shaking his head, while Phillips coughed. An approving murmur followed from the gallery. Otto smiled his thanks to the judge, and then continued.

"In view of the accused's plea, the state will not call any further evidence. I ask Your Honour to punish the accused according to the law, taking into consideration the great seriousness of the crime they have committed, and heavy punishment provided therefore." He drew out his final words as he added emphatically, "According to Old Roman Dutch Law."

The effect of Otto's words was immediate on both Wessels and all the accused, who instantly replaced their newspapers and sat bolt upright. Wessels stared hard at Otto, then immediately went into consultation with the accused and Barnato, as heads nodded in agreement.

Gregorowski took advantage of the lull. "It seems an opportune moment for the court to adjourn until three o'clock this afternoon." A babble of voices rose from the public gallery as he picked up his law books and stepped down from his bench. Those present also rose, their chairs scraping noisily on the wooden floor.

Shocked, Phillips shook his head, gazing wide-eyed at Kate, who was approaching. "We've been played!" She stopped for a moment with an angry expression hovered over her face as her eyes flashed. "My God, when *haven't* you been played!"

A pile of legal documents and case books full of precedents were stacked in front of the defence counsel as Judge Gregorowski indicated to them to proceed.

"Your Honour." Wessels addressed the judge directly. "I will be as brief as possible, but the case is of such an involved nature that I cannot give any hope of finishing within the hour."

"In spite of the plea, Advokaat Wessels?" the judge inquired, with raised eyebrows.

"I'm afraid so, Your Honour. Here we have a case in which Messrs Phillips, Farrar, Hammond and du Plessis plead guilty to a charge of high treason on the first count. I would like to discuss the question of law so that we may see not only what the law is, but which law it is." He paused, allowing the murmurs to subside, then continued. "Must we go back to the Old Roman Dutch Law, or must we follow our local laws?"

Smiling confidently at the crowded courtroom, he opened two volumes, letting the sound reverberate around the hopeful room. "According to Moorman and Voet, if local law imposes a lesser punishment for serious crime than Roman Dutch Law, the law imposing the lesser punishment should be applied."

Hushed whispers circulated among the crowd as Wessels readdressed the judge. "Now, Your Honour, the Afrikaners are not a bloodthirsty or vindictive people. The people of the Republic have published in their law books their humane view concerning the punishment for high treason."

He pushed his glasses over the bridge of his nose as he pointed to both case books. "Compare the 33 Articles, namely articles 9a and 10 which provide for a fine of 500 Rix dollars in cases of conspiring with foreign powers against the state, or for acting in a traitorous manner. I submit, Your Honour," he whipped off his glasses. "That the *mens rea* legislation in this Republic is that banishment and monetary fines shall be the only punishment for high treason."

Angry cries emanated from the public gallery denouncing his argument as he tried to continue. He raised his voice above the outcry. "If there is any doubt as to whether the punishment of death still survives, then the judge should rather follow Voet. *Peonas milliendas quam exasperandas.*"

While everyone was trying to work out the meaning of the Latin axiom, Hammond nudged Francois. "Look at that guy from the Volksraad Committee."

The object of their attention smiled knowingly and shook his head.

"Do you think we ought to protest?" Hammond whispered.

"Wouldn't do any good," Francois replied. "Gregorowski is also shaking his head."

Wessels continued. "Jameson came in as a private citizen. The clause in 33 Articles referring to treason deals specifically with conspiracy with foreign powers so it cannot be applied. Only a lesser form of punishment will be appropriate."

A sour expression of disagreement formed on Gregorowski's face as he shook his head in the direction of the members of the Volksraad Committee who smiled back appreciatively.

"I observe that this argument does not appear to impress Your Honour, nor some of our distinguished guests." Wessels commented, diverting from his legal train of thought as he focused on the Volksraad members.

"Advokaat Wessels," Gregorowski leaned forward. "I am under the impression that in this case, the accused did conspire with a foreign power to come into the country and take away its independence. If the accused had not conspired with Jameson in the first place, he would not have come into the Republiek at all."

"With respect, Your Honour, this is not so," Wessels argued indignantly.

"Whatever the intention of Cecil Rhodes or Chamberlain might have been, or that of Jameson and his men, the Reform Committee had nothing to do with it. Those people," as he pointed in the direction of the men on trial, "might have been using the accused for their own ends, but they did not know it."

He let his words sink in by pausing before continuing. "At least, not at that time. They probably know it now. In fact, they had everything to lose by conspiring with the Chartered Company." He looked around the courtroom. "Your Honour, the sword of justice has been entrusted to you. You can use it in two ways, severely and thereby cause bitter feelings and a revival of racial hatred among the inhabitants of this state. Or, you can use it mercifully and restore the country to its former state of peace and happiness."

Applause burst forth from among the small group of Uitlander onlookers as he resumed his seat. Others jeered as Gregorowski hammered his gavel in vain. It took a good few minutes until the public gallery grew silent.

Now, Otto stood up impatiently. He displayed mounting agitation. Before he could speak, Wessels leapt to his feet. "Your Honour, if it is my learned friend's intention to address the court again, I must protest that in all my experience I have never known such a thing to happen except under the most unusual circumstances. I have been pleading for mercy. It is unheard of that the prosecutor for the state should get up, as it were, and try to press home the charge vindictively."

Gregorowski opened his mouth to reply, but before he could utter a sound, Otto growled. "Counsel for the defence has given his interpretation of the law. Now I will give mine." His face had a forbidding expression. "He has quoted from various authorities regarding the administration of justice in this country. According to van der Linden, the punishment for sedition is," he paused to emphasise his words, "*hangen by den nek!*"

Kate's hands flew up to her mouth covering her shocked expression. Wessels stared back at Otto, astonished and disgusted. The prisoners' faces reflected equally stunned looks as the gravity of his words struck home.

Otto took a long swallow of water before continuing. "My duty here is strictly to interpret the law of the land. It is for this court to apply that law. The Volksraad Council under the President is there to reduce the sentence if they consider it too severe. I can only demand that the accused are punished with the full severity of the law. The court is well aware of what that punishment is. However, I may add that in Mynheer du Plessis' case, there may well be extenuating circumstances since as a Boer, he helped capture Jameson. " He sat down abruptly; his grim face flushed.

A heavy silence permeated the courtroom as Gregorowski noisily cleared his throat. "I need time to peruse the documents handed in during the trial. I will, therefore, adjourn until eleven o'clock tomorrow morning." Tucking a bundle of notes under his arm, he nodded to the gallery, then left.

A knocking on the courtroom door heralded the judge's re-appearance the next morning. Those present rose. A hushed, eerie silence fell over the courtroom as his footsteps echoed on the wooden floor.

He smiled to members of the Volksraad and nodded in greeting to Otto. He sat down and rustled some papers while the prisoners looked at him tensely. "I have carefully considered the statements made by all the accused," he commented. "Article 31 of the Transvaal has been quoted in support of the Counsel's contention that the only penalty for high treason is banishment and a fine of 500 Rix dollars. In van der Linden, it is stated that the Old Roman Dutch Law should be applied unless a special provision is made by an Act of the Volksraad. I do not think the Article has reference to cases where a foreign foe is actually brought to this country by the action of the inhabitants."

He re-examined his notes. "Therefore, the punishment laid down in the 33 Articles cannot apply if the state is under the impression that no extenuating circumstances exist. I am prepared to reserve that point for a decision of the full bench." He broke off as he gazed across at the prisoners. Now he took a deep breath. "I have said all that I consider necessary regarding the facts and the law in this case. It is my duty to pass sentence on the accused."

He beckoned to the Head Jailer who nodded across at the end of the prisoners' enclosure. He tapped each of the men on the shoulder. They stood up and faced Gregorowski, the man who had the power of life or death over them. The tension was palpable, and not a murmur could be heard around the expectant courtroom. Francois smiled weakly at

Kate. He too was jittery.

"Lionel Phillips," the judge began. "Have you any legal reason to urge why the sentence should not be passed upon you."

"No," Phillips replied, distinctly worried.

The same question was asked of George Farrar, John Hays Hammond and Francois du Plessis. All answered in the negative.

The judge then passed sentence on the other prisoners, who were the rank and file of the Reform Committee, condemning them to two years' imprisonment or fines of £2,000 each. The alternative was another year's imprisonment, and after that, be banished from the state for three years. Solly Joel, Barnato's nephew, was among those convicted.

"Lionel Philips, George Farrar, John Hays Hammond and Francois du Plessis, it is my painful duty to pass the death sentence upon you." His voice was stern and cold. "Although there may be extenuating circumstances concerning Mynheer du Plessis as he helped capture Jameson and he's a Boer. I leave that to the President."

A gasp of shock came from Kate. The room seemed to spin in front of her. Some of the Boers cheered. "I will leave it to his Honour, the President and the Volksraad Council to show you mercy which is in their power. May the great benevolence shown by his Honour and the government to the whole world during the recent painful events also be shown to you." He pulled out a black cloth cap and put it on. He clutched a Bible aloft in the other hand and continued in a dour tone. "The sentence of this court is that you remain in jail in Pretoria until the time and place of execution is fixed. There you will be hung by the neck until you are dead! May Almighty God have mercy on your souls."

A sigh of dread permeated the court. Murmurs of disbelief escaped the lips of the accused. Shocked to the core, Kate slumped forward in a faint as Barnato released his grip on her. He rose to his feet and gripped the railing. Spittle frothed from his mouth as he screamed above the din.

"Kaffir lawyer hired to do the government's dirty work! You know who I am Gregorowski, and I know you! You were always a rotten lawyer, and you've become worse since you were promoted," He ranted. "You know why you're here? Because no decent man would take on this sort of job. So, they found you!" He jabbed an accusatory finger at the judge. "The only man low enough to do the job the government wanted doing. You should have stayed in your tin-pot court in Bloemfontein where you only had weaklings to deal with. Kaffir lawyer, that's what you are!"

A stunned silence precipitated Gregorowski's reply as everyone remained rooted to their seats. " Mister Barnato, you are no gentleman!" His voice boomed. "I was appointed to put down the rebellion, and I have done so to the best of my ability!"

"Gregorowski, you are no judge," Barnato retorted, his voice edged with scorn.

"You had better quieten down, or you'll be had up for contempt of court," the judge threatened.

"Just try," Barnato replied haughtily. Then he turned to the four accused. "Don't worry boys. I'll have you out of there in no time."

Moving away from his seat, he strode over to the dock and grabbed hold of Francois' sleeve. "Come on, Francois, we're wasting our time in this here crackpot court. We have to visit Kruger."

The guard hesitated, uncertain as to what he should do; then he stepped in front of Francois who promptly pushed him aside as he stomped towards the door.

"Where the hell do you think you are going?" Gregorowski shouted. "You're a prisoner!"

A surging rage surfaced from deep within Barnato as he showed his strength. He grabbed the larger judge by the shoulder and propelled him straight at the closed window. Glass shattered in all directions. Instantly, one of the guards raised his rifle and took aim at Francois. He halted in his tracks and watched Barnato march out.

Barnato paused in his stride as he passed the injured judge whose dazed and bloody eyes looked up at him. "Next time you see me," he hissed contemptuously, "you'd better get out of my way and stay out."

The guards gathered around Otto as they watched Barnato storm down the Pretoria road. Nobody stopped him.

Barnato fumed as he paced back and forth outside Kruger's stoep waiting for the President to appear. His way was blocked by a group of Boers. He waited a full two hours before they ushered him inside where Kruger stood, steely-eyed. He spurned Barnato's outstretched hand. Without motioning him to be seated, Kruger confronted him.

"You are lucky that I have received you. It is against my better judgement and only because of our good relations in the past that I have allowed it, Mynheer Barnato." He glowered at Barney. "Your behaviour this morning was not only an insult to the judge but an affront to the state and to me personally."

"It was never meant to be such, Mr President," Barnato replied, somewhat chastened. "My first duty is to apologise to you as President, and through you to Judge Gregorowski and the court. I was shocked at the harshness of the sentences, and my behaviour was because of that shock. They did not take me into their confidence even though they knew my views."

"In that case, I accept your apology." There wasn't a hint of a smile on the elderly statesman's face. "Shall we say you were not yourself this morning."

"I am grateful, Your Honour." Barnato appeared relieved. "But that does not alter my opinion that the sentences were not only harsh but wicked."

"Bah," Kruger snapped. "You are always, tap, tap, tapping at the tail of the snake. Why don't you just cut his head off? Go for Rhodes, the chief offender, rather than coming to worry me." He drummed his fingers noisily on the leather casing of his Bible. "Where is Rhodes? I'd like to strangle him. Remember the sentences were accordance to the law, which is not evil, Mynheer Barnato."

"Then, they are foolish. You can't carry them out. If you did, the Republic wouldn't last twenty-four hours," he warned. "There will be no Reform Committee to hold back the Uitlanders. They would get immediate support from England and America too." He prodded a finger at the President. "Every mine and business enterprise on the Witwatersrand would close overnight, and then where would the Republic be?"

"Wealth cannot break laws," Kruger retorted. "The Uitlanders and you yourself, Mynheer Barnato, are too fond of money to take such action. You ask yourself where would we be. I ask, where would you be?"

Barnato half-smiled to himself as he breathed deeply. He swayed to and fro on the balls of his feet, with his hands stuck in his trouser pockets. "You don't believe me? Very well, then Mr President. I'll prove it to you. Unless the death sentences are commuted, and all sixty-four members of the Reform Committee released from jail in two weeks, I shall shut down every single one of my companies in the Transvaal!"

Kruger stared back at him, an expression of both annoyance and disbelief evident on his face. "Do you realise what that will mean?" Barnato continued as he drove home his advantage. "I employ thousands of whites and blacks. If I shut up shop, I'll throw more people out of work than you have burghers. The 50,000 pounds a week my companies spend in the Republic will be lost to you." His tone became more aggressive. "Already as a result of the crisis, the production of the gold mines has dropped by twenty million tons." His eyes blazed. "Do you want me to ruin your country, Mr President? I mean what I say. Wait and see!"

A gleam of disbelief glinted, and then faded from Kruger's eyes. "I do not make the laws, Mynheer Barnato, nor can I break them. What you have said will be reported to the Volksraad Committee."

"The men who are languishing in prison can't wait for your burghers to learn sense." Barnato's mouth was set in a thin, pursed line. "I'll give you another fortnight from now, and that's the last concession I'll make." Turning, he strode from the room, leaving a troubled President behind him.

"Extra! Intended sale of all Barnato properties. Extra!" shouted the newspaper boy outside the Volksraad, and his voice echoed through the chamber. The unwelcome news caused a momentary halt in the heated discussion.

"I think we should act leniently with them," Kruger continued.

"Why?" Otto interrupted. "Remember what they did to us at Slachter's Nek!"

Kruger spat out the name. The Raad members cautiously watched the confrontation. "Where they hung our people. Has that damned place not been the cause of so much trouble for the last 80 years?"

Otto gazed around the Raad, seeking members' approval. "Ja, Mr President, and that's why we should remember it."

"Who could forget it?" Kruger reflected. "All you *Raadslede* know what happened and yet you want to start another Slachter's Nek now. What is the use of whipping the little dogs when the big one is out of reach?"

He glared at the members. "I say, let them pay for the damage they caused the Republiek, then let them get out of the country!" He paused, the added forcefully, "Do not forget the grave warning that lies in the words, 'divide and rule'. Never let these words apply to the Republiek. With solidarity, our people and our language will endure and prosper."

Johannesburg

Following the Jameson Raid in December 1895, the members of the Reform Committee were charged with high treason. The ringleaders were sentenced to death in April 1896, later commuted to fifteen years' imprisonment. In June 1896, all members of the committee were released on payment of a hefty fine.

An agreement was reached, and Barnato paid the Reform Committee fines totalling over one million pounds to get all the men released. He had not only secured the future of the gold mining industry but saved the lives of those sentenced to death, possibly more. The conditions in the Transvaal prison could have killed a number of those with lesser sentences.

Uitlanders gathered joyously outside Hammond's office, their diggings temporarily abandoned as they chanted. "We want Barney!" A rousing welcome greeted him when he finally appeared on the balcony.

"Well my friends, it's good to hear you cheering the government of this country." He allowed the laughs to subside before continuing. "It's been a long time since we've been able to do that, and I hope it won't be the last!"

Spontaneous cheers erupted and were followed by shouts of "Good old Barney!"

He wallowed in their admiration. "By the way, the drinks are on me this evening."

The air was filled with ecstatic whoops of delight as Barnato waved back.

"With regard to the Reform leaders, their sentences have been commuted to a fine of 25,000 pounds sterling each. Don't worry, I'll pay it. Furthermore, the sentence of banishment commences immediately upon their release. It will not be enforced upon those who give their word of honour in writing that they will not intervene with the politics of the Republic in the future."

Barnato acknowledged the jeers which turned to cheers and rose to a crescendo as Phillips, Farrar, Hammond and Francois entered onto the balcony. They waved, smiled and laughed at the response of the crowd and held their hands aloft in victory.

Phillips stepped forward and held his hand out for silence. The gathering hushed. "We wouldn't like you to think that you've played no part in this decision, but we don't believe there's anything to be gain by emphasising this aspect of the situation." His voice rang out. "We propose that a delegation be appointed to give a formal expression of our gratitude to the President. So, give me three cheers for Paul Kruger. Hip, hip, hooray!"

Kruger decided, as an act of humiliation to Rhodes and the British government, to send the swarthy good-looking Leander Starr Jameson and his raiders back to Britain to stand trial. Upon their arrival they were feted as heroes.

Kruger despised Rhodes, considering him corrupt and immoral, calling him "capital incarnate" and "the curse of South Africa". He duly also published the correspondence between Rhodes and Jameson, exposing their plotting to the world. This afforded Kruger the moral high ground, and for the next few years international sympathy lay with the Transvaal.

Rhodes was forced to testify, presenting a wretched figure he cut during the two days he was in the witness box. Jameson was given a fifteen-month sentence, serving only six months in London before returning to South Africa. The Transvaal government was paid almost one million pounds in compensation by the British South Africa Company. Incredibly, Jameson was later knighted, and served as Prime Minister of the Cape for four years, while Rhodes was forced to resign as Prime Minister of the Cape Colony.

England's objective was simply to rob South Africa's minerals from the Boers. The English Press said in *The Indian Planters Gazette*: "the Boers must be exterminated like contaminated rats". They believed that if the Transvaal Republic was left to grow financially, it would eventually grow in size and topple Britain from its position of power in South Africa.

People like Phillips, Farrar, Robinson, Fitzpatrick, Beit and Bailey were directors and staff of the Rand Goldmine companies. They were very aware of the millions that they would get if the Transvaal would lose its independence.

CHAPTER 19

Yet in Africa's great future
Still we live in Trekkers' fame
Children of the nation will flourish
Bearers of an honoured name.

Pretoria

They sat on chairs under the warm, summer, star-studded Highveld sky, their attention riveted on the stage before them. General Piet Otto sat next to Francois, with Kate and Josh on his left. They were all engrossed watching a satire based on Jameson's raiders. The actors poked fun, causing great mirth and hoots of derisive laughter from the vast majority of the rough Boer audience.

"When shall we three meet again?" The actor who portrayed Phillips asked in an upper-class posh accent. "In London, Cape Town, or on the Rand?"

"When the dirty work is done, and the Transvaal has been won." A far more jocular Rhodes than the real one replied with a wink. "That will be an easy task, an invitation's all I ask. On your intrigue I'll depend: start sedition on the Rand and I from Bechuanaland at a signal will descend!"

The Jameson look-alike waved his hands about in a sweep of grandeur.

"Boers will fall before the raid, and our fortune will be made," added Phillips, rubbing his hands in gleeful anticipation of the profits.

The stage lights dimmed. Jameson exited as the pseudo-Barnato tripped purposefully onto the stage. Twirling a cane, he approached Phillips. "I understand that your movement promises success. I'd like to join. What can I do?"

"The best service you can give is to subscribe," Phillips replied.

"Good, a name is what I crave."

"A name is what he needs," Phillips added in an aside to the audience.

"Well, 10,000 pounds I'll give provided that you keep the record of it a secret until the new Republic is formed."

"Agreed," Phillips replied as Barnato handed him the cheque.

"Now I'm a revolutionary. This is the proudest moment of my life!" He approached the audience, then with a skip and a twirl of his stick, he raised his top hat and began singing . . .

As I walk through Throgmorton Street
with an independent air,
You'll hear the folks declare
there goes the millionaire.
You should hear them sigh and almost die
with envy as they loudly cry
The man to start a bank is Barney Barnato."

He knelt on one knee, hands spread, waiting for applause.

"How shall I secrete the record of Mr Barnato's subscription?" Phillips turned and asked Rhodes.

"Hide it under Barnato's hat. No one would think of looking there for anything."

Laughter spilt over as Phillips and Barnato exited. Jameson re-entered, paper and pencil in hand, as he strolled around the stage. "Whatever I write, they'll blame me. It will make them howl and hiss. So, I think it very gamely to immortalise rot like this."

"How is the ode coming on?" Rhodes asked.

"It's nearly finished. Would you like to hear it?" Jameson answered with a twinkle in his eye.

"No, I have trouble enough of my own," Rhodes sighed. "Oh well, if I must, I must."

"Wrong? Is it wrong?" Jameson began. "Most wickedly wrong," Rhodes retorted to the audience. Their mocking laughter rang in his ears. "But I'm going all the same."

"That treacherous raid," Rhodes whispered. "They may argue and babble and order. Go tell them to save their breath." Rhodes now dangled his legs over the stage with his back to Jameson as he faced the audience. "They may argue and hunt for excuses to prove their intention was good."

"There are girls in the golden city," Jameson continued.

"Also, a swell bunch here at the Alhambra," Rhodes commented.

"There are mothers and children too!"

"Strange coincidence," snorted Rhodes. The audience laughed in unison.

"And they cry, hurry up!"

"Gee up tishy."

"For pity."

"Of this ditty."

"We were wrong!" cried Jameson.

"Sob, sob," cried Rhodes, drawing out his handkerchief and wiping his eyes. The audience clung to every word.

"But we aren't half sorry."

"Not half," Rhodes replied as the public broke into spontaneous laughter.

"And, as one of the baffled band."

"Raffles?" Rhodes asked aside.

"I would rather have had the foray," Jameson exclaimed proudly puffing out his chest.

"Good old Rob Roy!"

"Than the crushing of all the Rand. Well, what do you think of it?" enquired Jameson, beaming.

"It requires no thought. It confirms my belief that you were made, not born. So, hurry the ode along. We want to have it ready to spring upon an unsuspecting public as soon as you cross the Transvaal border. I shall send a cable denouncing your raid and shall warn you to return. But you will not receive it in time to interfere with our anti-Transvaal plans. So, haste your awful rhymes and write me down a hero. Your crime will draw the public gaze from mine to yours." Jameson exited with a smile as another actor playing Percy FitzPatrick walked on stage.

"You were the secretary of the Reform Committee?" Rhodes probed.

"Yes." The actor nodded. His reddish wig shook with the movement." To what do you attribute the failure of the cause?"

FitzPatrick scratched his head before answering as the lights played on his face. "To the absence of the Irish. You can't ferment a successful revolution without the aid of the Irish."

"Did you read Jameson's ode?" Rhodes asked.

"Yeah, but the night after, I had a terrible dream."

"What was it about?"

"I dreamt I was reading it again."

The audience continued to roar with laughter as the skit ended.

The night was warm with the perfumed scent of honeysuckle. Kate and Francois, flanked by Josh and Otto, strolled arm in arm slowly down the jacaranda avenue away from the theatre.

"If only they could have all been here tonight," Kate sighed.

"Haven't you heard that Barney drowned at sea?"

"Or maybe he was pushed?" Francois' voice was filled with sadness. He missed the vibrant Cockney.

"Do you think it was suicide?" Otto questioned.

"No, I don't believe it was suicide. It was that bastard nephew of his who he brought on as a partner, who smacked him and then tossed him overboard. Then his other nephew mysteriously dies, and now this 31-year old Solly Isaacs has stolen Barney's company and fortune. The rumour is that Barney caught him embezzling and was taking him to England where he was going to expose him."

"But the papers say suicide, although they also predict another war."

"Can you believe them?" Otto raised his thick bushy eyebrows.

Francois stared quizzically at him. "But Piet, I always thought you wanted war!"

"Many people think that, but they are wrong. Let me tell you, never does a day or night pass without me thinking what a war would mean to our people, and to me. It would ruin South Africa! Just think of it, from my point of view. I am one of four brothers; one of them has already been killed in a South African war. The others might be killed in this one. Now, supposing I had a brother of one of my most valued friends killed and I was guilty of deliberately provoking the war. I would be the murderer of my friend's brother too." He glanced at Francois. "I'm afraid you're an optimist. I don't want war, but I am certain that it is coming."

Josh kicked a stone out of the gravel roadway as they strode the next few paces without speaking.

"You know, Piet," Francois nudged him. "I've got a strong feeling that the last thing Milner or Chamberlain wants is for Kruger to be defeated in the upcoming election."

Puzzled, Otto stopped and caused Francois to jolt Kate's arm.

"Why on earth should you think that? If Burger and his Progressives get power, half the problem will be solved. There'll be reduced taxation on the mines and franchise concessions."

"And that'll help to keep the Republic intact?" Francois enquired and raised a questioning eyebrow.

"Of course, it will. What . . .?" He stopped abruptly in mid-sentence, as the implicit meaning filtered through his mind.

"That's the whole point, Piet." Francois prodded his index finger in the air. "That's why I believe Chamberlain would prefer Kruger to be re-elected. There will be no concessions from the stubborn old goat."

"But that will lead to intervention." Otto retorted, wide-eyed.

"Exactly!" Francois replied.

"What do you think will really happen, General?" Kate asked as she uncoupled her arm.

Otto sighed, and then stared fixedly at the starry sky. "I see two great thunderclouds approaching. When they meet, there will come the crash and deluge."

"But don't you think Kruger should give the franchise to the Uitlanders?"

"*Ag*, I know that he's wrong and I tell him so. But first, he argues with me, and if that's no good, he gets into a rage and jumps around the room, roaring at me like a wild beast so that I cannot hear myself talk." Otto nodded at their incredulous looks on their faces. "And if I do not give in, he fetches the Bible, and *ach du Liebe Gott*, he even quotes that to help him out. And if that fails, takes my hand and cries like a child. Then he begs and prays for me to give in. Who could resist such a man?"

"Hell! If I were Kruger," quipped Kate smiling cheekily, "I would give the vote to the Uitlanders, but I would do the counting."

They all chuckled continuing along the footpath. The sweet aroma of the blossoming purple jacarandas was pungent.

"Funny," Francois added, "three years ago they raided, and everybody said they were wrong. Now the Queen's government is preparing another raid, and everyone says they're right."

Otto flashed a warning smile over at Francois. "If you and your Uitlander friends are at the bottom of this trouble, I will catch you someday, and this time no consideration will be given to personal friendship. The day I catch you, I'll hang you as high as Haman. You can count on that."

A half-smile creased Francois' lips. "You'll never catch me because I'm not guilty of what you think."

Otto laughed gruffly. "Ja, you can bluff as much as you like, but I know you are behind it."

Vultures wheeled above with the stench of battle polluting the air. The hot sun burnt the skin of the rooinek English soldiers, adding to their discomfort. Nearby, remnants of the Boer-British engagement lay strewn over the battlefield as British militia men picked their way past dead horses searching for survivors and collecting bodies for burial.

A corporal led the youth forward at gunpoint. Before the table, flanked by a lieutenant displaying the Duke's insignia, sat the British colonel flanked by his lieutenant. "What," he barked. "You caught only him? What about Otto and du Plessis?"

"They got away, sir, "the lieutenant meekly replied as he stood to attention, avoiding eye contact.

"Again?" The colonel bellowed angrily. "How could they! We had them surrounded!"

"I'm sorry, sir, they slipped away during the ambush. You know du Plessis is a wizard at bush craft."

The colonel shook his head wearily and sighed, then turned his attention to the young man. "All right, we've got them on the run now, we'll still capture them. Who's the youngster?"

"The lieutenant, realising the rebuke was over, snapped out. "Pisani, Josh Pisani, sir! He was with the Boers."

A puzzled look surfaced on the colonel's face as he tried to place the name. "Pisani! That's du Plessis' adopted son!"

"What are we going to do with him, sir?"

"I'm not sure. We've already captured du Plessis' wife and sent her to the concentration camp. Do you think du Plessis would come back for him? I wonder." He smiled. "Get ready for a hanging parade."

"You can't hang me," Josh blurted out and struggled as the corporal grabbed hold of him. "I'm a prisoner of war!"

"Can't we sonny?" The colonel replied with a vicious grin. "You'll see. Take him away, corporal."

"What are you really going to do, colonel?" the lieutenant asked as Josh was led away at gunpoint.

"Look, if we hang the lad, du Plessis and maybe Otto will try to rescue him."

"But sir, he's only a youngster," the lieutenant protested.

"Too bad. Catching du Plessis and Otto are more important. It's the war, rather than one young man's life. Give Pisani a bottle of scotch and get the padre to give him the last sacraments. In the meantime, I'll prepare the men."

With guns gripped tightly and breath held hard, they watched every bush, tree and rock. They crouched down, not daring to move. Concealed in the thick foliage, Francois turned to Otto as they observed the camp spring into a hive of activity. A noose was being slung over the bough of a willow tree.

"What are we going to do, Piet?"

"There's nothing we can do, Francois. If we go for the boy, they'll get both of us. Let's face it, the Boers in the concentration camps need us more. There's simply no way out."

"The bastards!" Francois hissed.

"I'm truly sorry, Francois." Otto consoled him as they watched and waited.

"Look, what if I started a diversion to the left of those trees and draw their fire?" Francois suggested suddenly. "Do you think the rest of you could get Josh?"

Otto considered the idea for a moment. "Ja, we could try that, but they'll get you, Francois, and we need you."

"They'll get you." His comrade warned again.

Francois gave a boyish grin, then slowly crept off towards his left, making for the bushy undergrowth where the horses were hobbled. "Maybe not," he whispered, then he disappeared.

Inside the tent, Josh took another swig from the bottle as the padre looked on uncomfortably, knowing he wasn't accomplishing his life's work. Josh started to giggle uncontrollably. "I promise I'll never touch another *dop, dominie.*" The irony of his words hit home and pricked at the padre's conscience as he tossed the bottle away.

Josh reeled as the flaps of the tent were drawn aside. The sun's rays lit up the tent as two burly corporals entered and locked their arms with his as they led him off. His feet trailed along the ground as they were forced to drag him along. The padre brought up the rear.

The noose at the end of the rope hanging from the bough swayed in the light breeze. With his hands tied securely behind him, Josh felt the cart edge forward as the drum rolled. Anxiously, he stared around, first at the soldiers near the trees and then up at the sky. He gulped on a sob as his whole body became numb with fear.

"It's a hell of a day when a man has his first drink, and then he is hung!" He called out hoarsely to the padre, as the soldiers congregated silently, nearby, arms at the ready.

The drum rolled on as the sweating corporal placed the thickly coiled and knotted rope around Josh's neck, causing him to weep hysterically. "The rope's hurting my ears."

No one laughed as the men – with the exception of the driver of the horse cart, who remained motionless, sjambok in hand – backed away while the drummer ceased rolling his drum. The silence hung heavy as they all waited for the command.

Josh could feel his heart pounding. Sweat ran down his forehead and tears flooded his cheeks. His life was at an end.

"You want me? Come and get me!" A commanding voice boomed from among the undergrowth far to the right of the soldiers.

"Get him!" screamed the colonel as his men whirled around and took aim, firing wildly in the general direction of the voice. But not before Francois had slipped neatly between the frightened horses. Bullets whistled all about him, spraying up dirt.

Behind Josh, Otto crept silently forward and leapt onto the cart, slipping the noose from Josh's neck. Five of his men suddenly appeared, galloping like the wind, and firing rapidly into the bunched soldiers.

Otto hacked at the rope which bound Josh's hands. Together they leapt onto the two spare horses. Immediately the soldiers whirled round again, firing madly at them.

At that moment, Francois emerged from behind a clump of trees, gun blazing as some of the soldiers caught in the confused crossfire dived for cover. Josh and Otto galloped towards the safety of their men.

A fleeting smile of triumph swept across Francois' face as his alert eyes absorbed the confusion. They would fight their way–hit and run, not the rooineks' way on a battlefield where their shining red uniforms made them easy targets for the Boer sharpshooters. He shrank back, merging with the shadows, back towards his men. Once again, they had shown these invaders the spirit of the Boer. Josh was safe. He had kept his promise to Pisani.

AUTHOR'S NOTES

*Terminology such as *piccanin* and *Kaffir lawyer* in Barnato's outburst in court (taken directly from the reported trial), was in common use at the time. It is not the sort of language the author would normally use.

Anglo-Boer War outcome

England launched the Anglo-Boer War to conquer the two Boer republics and steal their diamond and goldfields. It lasted two and a half years (1899-1902) pitting 478,000 imperial troops against 87,000 republican burghers. Boer armies took the offensive and punished British forces by avoiding conventional engagements in favour of guerrilla warfare.

After the initial setbacks, the British commander, Lord Kitchener was brought in to lead the army and defeat the Boers. He viewed them as an inferior race to the British, "rock-spiders" to be crushed. He devised a scorched-earth policy against the Boer commandos and the rural population by burning over 30,000 Boer homesteads and killing their cattle.

Correspondence between Chamberlain and Kitchener suggests they were aware that they were committing mass genocide by kidnapping the Boer women, children and old men and placing them in unsanitary concentration camps where two-thirds died of diseases such as measles as well as starvation.

The official justification was humanitarian motives, namely that the camps were meant to house Boer dependents who would otherwise roam the veld as unprotected refugees. Kitchener considered the internment of these Boer dependants desirable from a tactical standpoint. He argued that they made "every farm ... an intelligence agency and a supply depot", and might, by their absence, induce a Boer surrender. Separate camps housed black Africans.

By the end of the war, an estimated 27,927 Boers (eighteen per cent of the Boer population) comprising 4,177 women, 22,074 children under sixteen (eighty-one per cent of the children) and 1,676 old men died of disease and malnutrition in these camps. At the same time, 14,000 blacks died in separate camps.

These figures are likely to be much higher as no proper records were kept. Figures of 40,000 – 50,000 for people of colour have been mentioned.

England has never acknowledged these war crimes, nor apologised to the Afrikaner nation. The upshot of this action would lead to bitterness and hatred to this day, such that the majority of the Boer population did not support England during World Wars I and II.

Following World War II, the Nationalist party, supported mostly by Boers, won the national election and took control once again, introducing their "*apartheid* policies", based on the dictum "never again".

It is still possible that Great Britain will be charged at the International Criminal Court at the Hague for war crimes for the international crimes of genocide, crimes against humanity, war crimes, and crimes of aggression, and or, a private class action launched on behalf of the dependents of those who died in the concentration camps.

Meanwhile, Leander Starr Jameson and his raiders returned to England ironically in triumph for their trial following the failed Jameson Raid (thirty men were killed) and were treated as public heroes. Jameson was subsequently knighted, became a baronet, and was rewarded in

1904 by becoming the Prime Minister of the Cape Colony.

KEY IDENTITIES

Cecil John Rhodes (5 July 1853–26 March 1902)

Cecil John Rhodes was a colonialist for the British Empire and took control of Rhodesia on its behalf, naming the country 'Rhodesia' in his name while he made his fortune in South Africa in diamond mining.

He was also a supporter of the British imperial plan to unite South Africa under British rule but was the scapegoat after the Jameson Raid. This defeat ruined Rhodes' political reputation in the Cape and lost him the enduring support of the Cape Afrikaner Bond. Despite England's behind the scene participation in the Jameson Raid, Rhodes was forced to resign as Prime Minister of the Cape Colony on 12 January 1897 due to his apparent involvement in the planning of and assisting in the raid. He and Alfred Beit also resigned as directors of the British South Africa Company. He retired to his small simple cottage on the coast at Muizenburg, Cape Town, where he died in 1902.

He bequeathed Groote Schuur to be the official residence for future premiers of a unified South Africa. The De Beers Group, which he founded, remains the leading diamond company in the world.

Stephanus Johannes Paulus "Paul" Kruger (10 October 1825–14 July 1904)

Kruger conducted the Jameson Raid affair so successfully that his prestige soared again. He was one of the dominant political and military figures in 19th-century South Africa, and President of the South African Republic (or Transvaal) from 1883 to 1900. Nicknamed *Oom Paul* (Uncle Paul), he rose to international prominence as the face of the Boer cause—that of the Transvaal and its neighbour, the Orange Free State—against Britain during the Second Boer War of 1899–1902.

He has been called an embodiment of Afrikanerdom and remains a controversial and divisive figure; admirers revere him as a tragic folk hero, while critics view him as the obstinate guardian of an unjust cause.

Kruger took part in the Great Trek as a child during the late 1830s. He had minimal education apart from the Bible, and believed that the Earth was flat. His most prominent roles were in the creation of the South African Republic, leading its commandos, and resolving disagreements between rival Boer leaders and divisions. In 1883, he was elected President and at that time, Britain recognised the South African Republic as a fully independent state.

Following the influx of thousands of predominantly British settlers with the Witwatersrand Gold Rush of 1886, these Uitlanders delivered almost all of the South African Republic's tax revenues but lacked civic representation; the Boer burghers controlled the government. The Uitlander problem and associated tensions with Britain dominated Kruger's attention for the rest of his presidency, and led to the Jameson Raid of 1895–96, and eventually, the Anglo-Boer War.

In 1900, Stephanus Paulus Kruger was forced into exile during the Anglo-Boer War. He died in Clarens, Switzerland in 1904.

Kruger was also involved in the establishment of the Kruger National Park, which remains one of the largest game reserves in Africa.

Barney Barnato (February 1851–June 1897)

Barnato was born in London with the name Barnet Isaacs. His Jewish family was poor – his father sold second-hand clothing, his grandfather was a rabbi, and he left school at fourteen to help support the family. He and his older brother Harry became entertainers.

His success at the Kimberley diamond fields brought him into conflict with Rhodes, who wanted to control the price of diamonds and use the money to finance his sweeping political ambitions in Southern Africa. Eventually, they formed a partnership, De Beers Consolidated Mining.

However, Barnato did not share the imperialist expansion ambitions of Rhodes, nor did Rhodes, an Oxford man, like his uneducated Jewish Cockney associate. Finally, Barnato sold his shares for £4 million (£4,9 billion today) just seventeen years after arriving penniless in the Cape.

By this stage, Barnato had brought his two nephews, Solly and Woolf Joel into his Barnato Diamond Mining Company. He also became a member of the Cape Parliament for Kimberley.

Now their battleground moved to the Johannesburg goldfields.

Having partially coordinated the release of the Reform Committee, Barnato received an invitation to Queen Victoria's diamond jubilee celebrations. Shortly before his departure in 1897, the chief accountant at Johannesburg Consolidated informed Barney that there was an irregularity in the accounts for an amount in excess of one million pounds. The accountant blamed his nephew, Solly Joel.

When Solly was confronted with the discovery, he denied it. But Barnato must have shown him the proof and ordered him to make it good to the company. Furthermore, he ordered Solly back to England, something that Solly had no intention of doing. The alternative was the threat of a trial and imprisonment, such that there was bad blood between Barney and Solly.

In June 1897, Barnato, his wife Fanny, their two young children and Solly left Cape Town for Southampton on the Union Castle passenger ship, the RMS Scot. One reason for Barney's voyage back to London was thought to be to disinherit Solly for the theft and his part in the failed Jameson Raid.

Officially Barney committed suicide by jumping overboard while temporarily insane, but there is circumstantial evidence that he may have been murdered.

Shortly after three o'clock on the afternoon of the 14th June 1897, as the ship neared Madeira, Barney seated on deck with Solly is said to have suddenly given "a spring" over the rail into the sea and drowned. There were only two witnesses at the inquest.

Solly Joel: "I threw out my hands to catch him, but only caught the back of his trousers, and he jumped over the side into the sea. I screamed 'murder', and saw the fourth officer, who was sitting dozing, and said, 'For God's sake save him.'"

The other witness was William Tarrant Clifford, the fourth officer: "I saw him leap overboard. I pulled off my coat and jumped in after him. The body which was floating face down was picked up by the ship's boat."

Barney's grand-daughter, Diana Barnato Walker (who was the first British woman to break the sound barrier), states she was told by her cousin Stanhope (Stan) that Solly "gave him the heave-ho overboard". Stan was Solly's son.

Several unanswered questions arise:

As there was no post-mortem, how was it established that death was caused by drowning?

Why was the body floating so soon after drowning? This indicates there may have been air, rather than water, in the lungs.

Why did Solly shout "murder" rather than something like "help"?

Solly said that the fourth officer (Clifford) was dozing. If so, how did Clifford see Barney "leap" rather than just see Solly "catch" the back of Barney's trousers after the shout roused him?

Solly stated that he had received a telegram from Mrs Fanny Barnato asking him to come to Cape Town because of Barnato's poor mental state. Upon his arrival, he found this to be true which was why he left with Barnato. However, Fanny Barnato, who did not attend the inquest, subsequently denied that she sent this telegram and that Barney was in bad health, mentally or physically.

Furthermore, as Barnato was fabulously wealthy;

Why did the inquest proceed without Fanny Barnato, given that she was travelling with Barney, and that she was purported to have sent Solly a telegram alluding to Barney's state of mind?

Why was there no post-mortem for such a famous person?

Once Fanny Barnato both denied both sending Solly a telegram and that he was in a poor mental state, why was Barnato's body not exhumed and an autopsy performed?

Additional facts:

Barnato was at the height of his career, financially well-off, had a young family, and acclaimed for the part he played in getting the Reform Committee members released from jail.

After the inquest, William Tarrant Clifford was rewarded by the Joels with a payment of £1,000 (£400,000 today) and was promised that they would "use all their great influence to further his advancement".

Clifford, the only other witness, was a good friend of Solly's and went shooting with him on his English estate.

Diana Barnato Walker said that Solly may have "biffed" Barney before pushing him overboard. (*If Barney was knocked unconscious, this could explain why his body was floating).

Solly was determined to get control of the South African companies, such that "it was said that Solly masterminded a phoney indictment of illicit diamond buying against his brother Woolf".

Barnato did not support the Reform Committee or the Jameson Raid. Solly was a prominent member of the Reform Committee and found guilty of high treason for his part in the Jameson Raid.

At this level, did money change hands? Was it because the British government played a role? Barnato had inside knowledge of the Jameson Raid and all those involved. Possibly they did not want the Colonial Secretary Joseph Chamberlain's role in directing and supporting Rhodes in the disastrous Jameson Raid exposed, especially given their sensitive international relationships following the praise heaped upon Paul Kruger by Germany, France and Holland following the attempted invasion.

Louis Cohen, Barnato's cousin, first partner in Kimberley, and well-known journalist was threatened with prosecution for libel action by Solly Joel's attorneys in 1899 after Cohen inferred that Solly was behind Barnato's death. This action never proceeded.

Nine months after Barney's death, in 1898, his other nephew Woolf Joel was shot dead by Karl Frederick Kurtze (went by the name of von Veltheim). Von Veltheim only received two years from a Boer jury (possibly due to anti-British and anti-Semitic feelings towards the deceased). Solly's son, Stanhope, however suggested that "Solly probably paid for von Veltheim's defence".

With Barney and Woolf now dead, Solly (only thirty-two) took effective control of the business, Johannesburg Consolidated Investments (JCI).

As a final postscript to this bizarre tale, more than twenty-five years after Barney was killed, a two-year investigation of JCI's books was achieved via court actions brought by Barney's family confirmed that shortly before Barney's death, Solly had "been diddling Barnato out of one million pounds". Solly was forced to pay the Barnato's side of the family £960,000 (£1 billion today) plus thirty years' interest.

Suicide...... or murder?

Throughout his life, Barney never forgot his roots and provided funds for various Jewish institutions in London, including his old school. Unlike Rhodes, Barnato still enjoys a good reputation and is well remembered by history.

Reform Committee

The Reform Committee was a sixty-four-member committee representing the grievances of Johannesburgers to the Paul Kruger government. After their arrest, the ringleaders John Hays Hammond, Lionel Phillips, George Farrar and Frank Rhodes, all of whom had signed an incriminating document (together with Percy FitzPatrick, Charles Leonard and Douglas Gilfillan) found with Jameson's raiders, were sentenced to be hanged. Kruger commuted the sentences such that they would spend fifteen years in prison, and later a reduced fine of £25,000. The remaining Reform Committee members were initially sentenced to two years in prison, but this was later reduced to a fine of $2,000 each.

The ringleader, Leander Starr Jameson was returned to London where he was sentenced to fifteen months in jail, of which he only served six months. The raiders were fined some £300,000.

The High Commissioner to the Cape Colony, Sir Hercules Robinson, and the Colonial Secretary, Joseph Chamberlain, the force behind Rhodes and Jameson managed to conceal their complicity and knowledge of the raid.

What became of the Reform Committee ringleaders?

Sir Lionel Phillips (6 August 1855–2 July 1936)

Hearing of the discovery of large diamond deposits in Kimberley, Phillips decided to seek his fortune and immigrated to South Africa. He arrived at the Kimberley diamond fields in 1875 having walked most of the way there from Cape Town. He worked for Joseph

Benjamin Robinson as a diamond sorter and soon after that went into partnership with Alfred Beit.

He was found guilty and sentenced to be "hung by the neck" for his participation in the Jameson Raid. This was later commuted, and he was banned for a period. However, he subsequently ignored a warning and published an inflammatory article in the *Nineteenth Century*, resulting in his being banished from the Transvaal by State Attorney Jan Smuts.

He was knighted, and in 1912, Phillips was created a baronet. On 11 December 1913, while on his way to the Rand Club, he was shot at five times, but survived the attack. He returned to South Africa in 1924 and settled on the farm Vergelegen near Somerset West.

John Hays Hammond (31 March 1855–8 June 1936)

An early advocate of deep mining, Hammond was employed by and given control of Cecil Rhodes' mines in South Africa. He made each undertaking a financial success by introducing vertical mining to the goldfields. He was the principal influence in planning and executing the Jameson Raid at Rhodes' direction.

Along with the other leaders of the Johannesburg Reform Committee, he was arrested and sentenced to be "hung by the neck", such that the U.S. Senate petitioned Kruger for clemency. He was later released after paying a large fine.

He returned to the United States where he was a close friend of President William Taft. In 1908, he was a candidate for Vice-President for the Republican party, which he lost, and later became a special U.S. Ambassador to the coronation of King George V.

His son, John Hays Hammond, Jr., patented over 400 inventions, and is widely regarded as the father of radio control, and developed a radio-controlled torpedo system for the navy.

Sir George Herbert Farrar (17 June 1859–20 May 1915 South West Africa)

In 1887, shortly after the discovery of gold on the reef, Farrar and his brothers established themselves in Johannesburg. Here he became one of the leading figures in the mining sector on the East Rand. His main creation was the formation of the East Rand Proprietary Mines (ERPM) as the controlling shareholder.

He was a member of the Legislative Assembly of the Transvaal and Leader of the Opposition. For his part in the Jameson Raid, he was sentenced to be "hung by the neck", but the sentence was commuted to a fine of £25,000.

During the Boer War, he was appointed a Major in the Kaffrarian Rifles and was awarded the Queen's South Africa Medal with four clasps. Farrar was knighted in November 1902 and created a baronet in 1911.

Following the end of the war, he became Chairman of the Chamber of Mines. Farrar was an enthusiastic supporter of importing poorly paid Chinese workers on three-year contracts, resulting in even further ethnic tensions on the reef.

Colonel Frank Rhodes (9 April 1850–21 September 1905)

He was found guilty and sentenced to be "hung by the neck" for his involvement in the Jameson Raid, later commuted to a fine of £25,000. As a punishment for his support of Jameson, the British Army placed Rhodes on the retired list and barred him from active participation in army business.

After his release from jail, he immediately joined his brother Cecil and the British South Africa Company in the Second Matabele War.

In 1898, he joined Field Marshal Earl Kitchener's Nile expedition as the war correspondent for *The Times*. During the Battle of Omdurman on 2 September, he was shot and severely wounded in the right arm.

For his services during that campaign, he was reinstated to the army active list. During the Second Boer War, Rhodes continued as a war correspondent and was trapped for the period in the Siege of Ladysmith and subsequently participated in the relief of Mafeking.

Sir James Percy FitzPatrick (24 July 1862-24 January 1931)

He was a leading member and secretary of the Reform Committee in 1895 acting as go-between the committee, Cecil Rhodes and Leander Starr Jameson.

He was charged with high treason and sentenced to two years imprisonment, but only served one year. He later became President of the Chamber of Mines.

At the outbreak of the Second Anglo-Boer War in 1899, FitzPatrick helped to establish the Imperial Light Horse Regiment. He acted as Official Adviser on South African Affairs to the British government and was knighted in 1902, and later appointed a Knight Commander of the Order of Saint Michael and Saint George.

In 1907, his most popular work, *Jock of the Bushveld*, largely based on his experience in the Eastern Transvaal, was published. He contributed to the establishment of the Johannesburg Zoo and setting up citrus farming in South Africa.

Later FitzPatrick and General J.B.M. Hertzog worked out an agreement that recognised English and Dutch as the official languages of the Union, and he was also responsible for the creation of the two-minute silence observed on Armistice Day.

Sir Johannes (John) Wilhelmus Wessels (1862–1936)

The Reform Committee's Afrikaans Advocate was famous for his legal judgements and the law books he wrote, some of which are still referred today at South African law universities.

His works include *The Status of the Uitlander* (1894), *History of the Roman Dutch Law* (1908), *Codification of Law in South Africa* (1927), and *The Law of Contract in South Africa* (1937).

After the end of the Second Boer War, the government of the newly-created British Colony of Transvaal established a Supreme Court of Transvaal in April 1902 with Wessels as one of three judges. When the Union of South Africa was established in 1910, he became a judge in the Transvaal Provincial Division, and later a judge of the Appellate Division from 1923-1932, and Chief Justice of South Africa from 1932-1936.

*In 1900, Master Johannes Wilhelmus Wessels, aged eleven months, died of measles in the British Bethulie concentration camp. This was possibly his son.

Jameson Raid: Consequence (29 December 1895–2 January 1896)

Company troops ("police" in the employ of Alfred Beit and Cecil Rhodes' British South Africa Company) and Bechuanaland policemen took part in the Jameson Raid against the Transvaal Republic over the New Year weekend of 1895-96 with the full knowledge of Joseph Chamberlain, the British Colonial Secretary.

Paul Kruger was the President of the republic at the time. The raid was intended to generate an rebellion by the mainly British expatriate workers (known as Uitlanders) in the Transvaal but was unsuccessful. The Reform Committee's efforts to assemble the Uitlanders for revolt faltered, partly because not all mine owners ("Randlords") supported Rhodes.

The raid was unsuccessful, and there was no uprising. Consequences included embarrassment for the British government, dividing Anglo-Boer sentiment in South Africa, simultaneously aggravating republican distrust, Uitlander agitation and imperial concerns. Cecil Rhodes was replaced as premier of the Cape Colony, Afrikaner dominance of the Transvaal with its gold mines was reinforced and it is asserted that this event assisted the start of the Anglo-Boer War (1899-1902). Ultimately, it was a factor in the establishment of the apartheid system in the Union of South Africa

In Rhodesia, Jameson's raid had depleted Matabeleland of many of its troops creating vulnerability for the entire territory. Recognising this weakness, and the dissatisfaction with the British South Africa Company, the Ndebele revolted during March 1896 in the First War of Independence, also known as the *First Chimurenga*, but better known to most of the world as the Second Matabele War. The Shona joined them shortly afterwards.

Huge numbers of European settlers were killed within the first few weeks of the uprising, and many more died in the next eighteen months. With few soldiers left to defend and support them, the settlers rapidly constructed a laager in the centre of Bulawayo. There were over 50,000 Ndebele waiting in the Matobo Hills and the settlers formed patrols to defend themselves under individuals such as Burnham, Baden-Powell and Selous. It was only in October 1897 that the Ndebele and Shona finally laid down their arms.

OTHER CHARACTERS

Louis Cohen (1854–1945)

Louis Cohen was Barnato's cousin. He arrived in Kimberley in 1872 aged seventeen and became Barney Barnato's first partner. Cohen would have been a very rich man had the partnership not dissolved before Barnato's stellar successes on the diamond fields.

Cohen knew all the successful magnates on the diamond fields prior to their success and couldn't resist recounting all their failings and scandalous business methods in his book about Barnato's dealings with the early pioneers, *Reminiscences of Kimberley*.

In 1914, Sir J.B. Robinson successfully sued him for perjury, preventing all but fifteen copies of the book being printed, and Cohen consequently spent two years in jail.

In 1964, Princess Ida Labia (Robinson's daughter) unsuccessfully sued this author's father for his original copy of *Reminiscences of Kimberley*.

Sir Joseph Benjamin Robinson (3 August 1840-30 October 1929)

Sir Joseph's rather forceful business tactics led to his being heavily criticised and earned him the title of "Old Buccaneer".

After the discovery of gold in the Witwatersrand district in 1886, Alfred Beit formed a partnership with him investing £25,000. Robinson purchased the Langlaagte and Randfontein estates, but Beit soon dissolved the partnership because of Robinson's temper and business methods.

On 27 July 1908, he became a baronet of Hawthornden and Dudley House, and in June 1922, he was nominated for a UK peerage but declined the honour. The recommendation by Prime Minister David Lloyd George was subject to much debate in parliament as Robinson was considered unsuitable for such an honour

Sir J.B. Robinson's death in 1929 caused a great scandal in South Africa and Britain upon discovery of the terms of his will. His personal fortune of £12 million was given to his heirs, except for one daughter, who only received a mere £2,000. He gave nothing to charity or the state.

Judge Reinhold Gregorowski (1856-1922)

Initially, he was a Judge in the Orange Free State. He became State Attorney in 1896 and presided over the trial of the Reform prisoners in Pretoria following the Jameson Raid, despite having no status in the Transvaal. He is remembered for the abnormal harshness of his rulings for all except Boers, and it is claimed that he came to the trial of the

Reformers with the full intent of stretching the law as far as possible to ensure conviction of the prisoners.

In his summary, he stated that the signatories of the letter of invitation to Dr Jameson were directly accountable for the loss of life, that is the burghers at Doornkop. This despite the fact that the Committee had offered to personally guarantee that if the government allowed Dr Jameson to enter Johannesburg unmolested, he would leave peaceably as soon as possible. Consequently, the judge set aside the special statutes of the State and passed the death sentence upon the prisoners under the Old Roman Dutch Law.

The Judge then sentenced the other members of the Reform Committee to two years' imprisonment and fines of £2,000 each, and after that, to be banished from the State for a period of three years.

After the Anglo-Boer war, he was not reappointed as a judge and returned to the bar. However, following the establishment of the Union of South Africa, he was appointed a judge of the Transvaal Provincial Division in 1913, and in 1914, headed the commission of enquiry into the death of General 'Koos' De la Rey.

General Jacobus Hercules (Koos) de la Rey (22 October 1847–15 September 1914)

De la Ray disapproved of Kruger's attitude to the Uitlanders and was against inviting armed conflict with Britain. Nevertheless, he helped to capture the Jameson raiders. *(*General Piet Otto's character in the book is loosely based on De la Rey).* When speakers in the Raadzaal called for war, De la Rey condemned the action as premature, unsound and unnecessary. Angrily Kruger denounced his attitude as cowardly. Despite this, he served as a Boer general and was recognised as a hero for his actions during the Anglo-Boer War.

At the peace conference in 1902, he stated that he and his men were determined not to give up their independence, but with everything lost, it seemed futile to waste more lives when their survival as a country was at risk. After the war, he returned to rebuild his life on his devastated farm. During the war years, his wife and family had wandered from place to place in an effort to avoid capture.

De la Rey broke with Prime Minister Botha over supporting the British at the outbreak of World War I and openly communicated his wish for the restoration of the Boer Republic. Two days after voting to support Britain, parliament decided to invade German South West Africa. The burghers hoped De la Rey would call on them to rebel, and he was on the way to announce he was leading this uprising against the invasion. On 13 September, while evading the authorities, he was shot and killed at a police roadblock. Judge Gregorowski headed up the commission of enquiry which controversially determined his death was 'accidental'.

www.ingramcontent.com/pod-product-compliance
Lightning Source LLC
Chambersburg PA
CBHW032336300426
44109CB00041B/1063